W9-BEF-147

THE PULLMAN STRIKE
AND THE
LABOR MOVEMENT
IN AMERICAN HISTORY

Other titles *in American History*

IN
AMERICAN
HISTORY

THE PULLMAN STRIKE AND THE LABOR MOVEMENT IN AMERICAN HISTORY

R. Conrad Stein

E ||| **Enslow Publishers, Inc.**

40 Industrial Road   PO Box 38
Box 398   Aldershot
Berkeley Heights, NJ 07922   Hants GU12 6BP
USA   UK
http://www.enslow.com

Library of Congress Cataloging-in-Publication Data

Stein, R. Conrad.
The Pullman strike and the labor movement in American history / R. Conrad Stein.
 p. cm. — (In American history)
Includes bibliographical references and index.
ISBN 0-7660-1300-6
1. Pullman, George Mortimer, 1831–1897. 2. Chicago Strike, 1894—Juvenile
literature. 3. Strikes and lockouts—Railroads—Juvenile literature. 4. Railroads—
History—Juvenile literature. 5. Labor movement—Illinois—Chicago—Juvenile
literature. [1. Chicago Strike, 1894. 2. Pullman, George Mortimer, 1831–1897.
3. Strikes and lockouts. 4. Railroads—History.] I. Title. II. Series.
HD5325.R12 1894 .C5758 2001
331.892'8523'0977311—dc21
                                        00-010955

Printed in the United States of America

10 9 8 7 6 5 4 3 2 1

To Our Readers: All Internet Addresses in this book were active and appropriate
at the time we went to press. Any comments or suggestions can be sent by e-mail
to Comments@enslow.com or to the address on the back cover.

Illustration Credits: Courtesy of the Chicago Public Library Collection,
pp. 80, 101; Courtesy of the Historic Pullman Foundation, pp. 10, 15,
16, 21, 23, 24, 26, 27, 34, 56, 57, 59, 64, 69, 76, 77, 97, 106, 111;
Enslow Publishers, Inc., p. 67; Library of Congress, pp. 32, 50, 62, 72,
92, 95; R. Conrad Stein, p. 112.

Cover Illustrations: Courtesy of the Historic Pullman Foundation;
Library of Congress.

★ CONTENTS ★

SETTING THE STAGE

On the evening of July 6, 1894, a crowd of six thousand men and women descended on a railroad yard just south of downtown Chicago. Some shouted curses, but most were curious neighbors lured by the excitement. Leaders of the throng marched onto railroad property, and a night of rampage began. A dozen or so people rushed toward long lines of parked railroad cars. Several men threw blazing torches into the open doors. A reporter from a newspaper called the *Inter Ocean* said, "They [the rioters] looked in the gloaming like specters [ghosts or phantoms], their lighted torches bobbing about. . . . Soon from all parts of the yard flames shot up and billows of fire rolled over the cars, covering them with the red glow of destruction."[1]

It was the most violent night of the strike that stunned the nation. Even when the fury finally diminished, the American people would never forget the great Chicago upheaval of 1894. It had started as a local labor dispute and escalated to a general railroad strike that tied up train service in twenty-seven states. More than just a clash between workers and their bosses, the

Pullman strike appeared to many Americans to be a war between rich and poor. This labor battle changed the American labor movement forever.

The events in Chicago offered high drama that could have been set to stage. The two principal characters in this drama were George M. Pullman, a brilliant businessman and self-made millionaire; and Eugene V. Debs, a bold labor leader. Other characters included the governor of Illinois, the attorney general of the United States, and a young lawyer who would soon become a national figure. The drama took place at the height of the Industrial Revolution, a period that transformed life in the United States. Its stage was the city of Chicago, a child of the Industrial Revolution.

In many ways, the Pullman strike story was a tragedy. Workers entered the conflict starving, and they were still starving when the strike finally ended. At least thirty people were killed, and three times that number were injured over several days of rioting. Property damage was estimated at $80 million, a staggering sum in those days. But the labor war alerted Americans to the grim fact that, while industrialization brought riches to a few and prosperity to many, it left millions of workers struggling in miserable poverty. Ironically, this bitter battle began in a unique village that was created to provide a happy and healthy life for workers. That village was the dream of a remarkable man named George Pullman.

Resolved: That the completion of the magnificent sleeping coaches marks a notable epoch in the history of railway travel and that the thanks of the entire traveling public are due to Mr. George M. Pullman, the originator of the sleeping car enterprise. . . .

—Federal Judge Thomas Drummond, speaking at an 1866 picnic held to honor George Pullman.[1]

2

A MAN AND HIS DREAM

The Product of an Age

The Industrial Revolution was a time when machines entered shops and farmers' fields and performed miracles. Aided by new machines, workers vastly increased their production of food, clothing, and other goods. The Industrial Revolution began in England in the 1700s and spread to the United States in the early 1800s. During the nineteenth century, machines transformed the United States from a nation of farms into an industrial giant.

George M. Pullman, born in 1831, was a product of America's machine era. Like many other Americans, he was thrilled when he saw his first hissing and steaming train engine. Railroads served as the arteries of the

George Pullman, as he looked in about 1890, when he was fifty-nine years old.

Industrial Revolution. Huge train engines, called iron horses, were the most exciting devices Pullman and the people of his time had ever seen. Before the railroads, the average American could expect to live and die and never travel more than fifty miles from his or her hometown. During Pullman's youth, silver rails promised to speed people magically to cities, seacoasts, snowclad mountains, and other undreamed of places.

Pullman grew up in the small town of Portland, New York. He was the third child in a family of eight. His father, James Lewis Pullman, was a carpenter. Though he was a dedicated worker, the elder Pullman could provide little beyond the bare essentials for his large family. George attended only a few years at a country school. In his teens, he went to work as a cabinet maker in a shop owned by his brother. But young George dreamed of grander projects.

In the early 1850s, the state of New York decided to widen the Erie Canal. Completed in 1825, the canal cut across New York State and connected the city of Albany with the city of Buffalo. The state advertised for contractors to move sheds and warehouses away from the banks of the canal in order to permit its widening. George Pullman seized the opportunity. He hired a crew of strong young men to pry houses from their foundations, place them on wagons, and cart them to a new location. Moving large houses from one place to another was a common practice in those days. Housemoving became Pullman's first true profession, and one that would prompt him to move to Chicago.

SOURCE DOCUMENT

THE IRON HORSE WITH THE WINGS OF WIND, HIS NOSTRILS DISTENDED WITH FLAME, SALAMANDER-LIKE VOMITING FIRE AND SMOKE, TREMBLING WITH POWER, BUT SUBMISSIVE TO THE STEEL CURB IMPOSED UPON HIM BY THE HAND OF MAN, FLIES FROM ONE END OF THE CONTINENT TO THE OTHER IN LESS TIME THAN OUR ANCESTRY REQUIRED TO VISIT A NEIGHBORING CITY. . . . TRULY IT MAY BE SAID THAT [WITH THE HELP OF THE RAILROADS] ALL THE PEOPLE OF THIS CONTINENT MAY BE MOLDED TO ONE MIND.[2]

When George Pullman was born, trains were still in their experimental stage. By the time Pullman was in his teens, some six thousand miles of track had been built and railroads linked many cities in the East. A few dreamers even dared to believe that trains would some day cross the continent. The excitement generated by railroads can be seen in this speech, delivered in 1846 to the House of Representatives by Congressman Charles W. Cathcart of Indiana.

Chicago: No city in history grew with such explosive energy. In 1800, Chicago was a marshlands on the banks of Lake Michigan and had no permanent residents. Less than one hundred years later, it was the second largest city in the country and one of the five largest cities in the world. A creation of the industrial age, Chicago was a factory town and a shipping center. Its shops churned out farm machinery, and its lake ports and railroad yards sent goods produced by farms to markets in the East.

When Pullman arrived in 1855, Chicago suffered from a major problem—mud. The city was built on a swamp produced by the meeting of the Chicago River and Lake Michigan. Because its land lay almost level with the lake, rain water did not drain away from the streets. A heavy rain turned Chicago into a sea of muck. Residents swore that on one rainy day they saw a horse and wagon sink out of sight right on Lake Street in the heart of downtown.

To fix the drainage problem, city leaders announced they would raise the streets four to seven feet higher than their present level. This meant that buildings must also be raised to put them even with the streets. Largest of the buildings was the five-story Tremont Hotel, which sprawled over an entire city block. No housemover wanted to risk the expenses involved in raising this enormous building—no housemover except the fearless George Pullman.

To lift the hotel, Pullman hired one thousand laborers and supplied them with jackscrews. The jackscrews were similar to carjacks, except that they worked by turning a large screw with a handle. Workers dug down below the building's foundation, attached heavy timbers there, and placed jackscrews under the timbers. By blowing a whistle, Pullman's foreman had the laborers turn the jackscrews slowly on his command. Inch by inch, the Tremont Hotel was raised without so much as breaking a pane of glass. The hotel and other housemoving projects netted Pullman $20,000, a tidy sum of money in the

1850s for a twenty-seven-year-old without a formal education.

A Palace on Wheels

As a young businessman, George Pullman traveled often. In those days an overnight train trip was a painful experience. Passengers sat on stiff wooden benches during the day. At night, a conductor put thin mattresses over the seats. Riders stretched out as best they could and covered themselves with their overcoats because the railroads provided no blankets. Passenger cars stank of coal fumes. Often the windows would not open, making them ovens in the summer. During winter months the cars were heated only by a smoky wood-burning stove. Sleep was next to impossible on the overnight runs, and as the railroads expanded, lengthy trips became the norm. In the late 1850s, even the fastest trains took three to five days to go from New York to Chicago.

During one of his brutally uncomfortable train trips, George Pullman lay half-awake, toying with a single idea. Why not give passengers a comfortable railroad car? Why not build a car whose seats could be converted into beds, allowing the people a restful night's sleep? Surely people would be willing to pay more for pleasant accommodations while taking a long train ride. Pullman tossed this possibility over and over in his mind. Eventually, he developed the idea and made a fortune.

In 1858, Pullman bought two passenger cars from the Chicago and Alton Railroad and worked to build sleeping facilities inside them. The project was not new. Others had tried to build sleeping cars. But none of the others had the single-minded determination of George M. Pullman. Using the skills he acquired as a cabinetmaker, Pullman devised a hinged seatback. The hinges allowed a porter to fold the seatback down to form a bed. An upper bed was attached to the car's ceiling with pulleys and lowered at night. That way, Pullman's sleeping cars had two rows of double-layered beds, upper and lower. Partitions placed between the beds gave sleeping passengers privacy. Pullman patented his bed-converting devices. In fact, sleeping

A newly built Pullman passenger car provided luxurious accommodations for customers.

This Pullman club car, built in the 1890s, included electric lights on the ceiling—a very modern touch for the times.

cars today still use the principles first devised by George Pullman.

Passengers were delighted with Pullman's sleeping cars, but at first railroad companies showed little interest. Some railroad men called the new cars "Pullman's Folly." In fact, Pullman himself was not satisfied with his product. He dreamed of giving passengers luxury along with beds at night. To accomplish this, he could not simply convert existing passenger cars. He had to build a new car from the tracks up.

The American Civil War (1861–1865) delayed Pullman's plans. The war was a bloody contest that pitted the slaveholding Southern states against the

Northern free states. Pullman favored the North. In 1864, as the war drew to a close, Pullman rented a railroad repair shed in Chicago and proceeded to build what he called the "biggest and best car ever."[3] Pullman named the new car the Pioneer, and a pioneer it certainly was. The Pioneer was a foot wider and more than two feet higher than existing railroad cars. The Pioneer cost more than five times as much to build as the passenger cars then in use. It was too tall to fit under existing bridges and too wide to be serviced by depot platforms then in use. But the giant car gave customers a smoother ride. Pullman said confidently, "This is what a sleeping car must have; the entire railroad system of America will be changed to fit its needs."[4]

A national tragedy gave Pullman a chance to display his creation. On the evening of April 14, 1865, just five days after the South surrendered, bringing the Civil War to a close, President Abraham Lincoln was shot and killed by the assassin John Wilkes Booth. The nation mourned as Lincoln's body was taken by train from Washington, D.C., to its final resting place in Springfield, Illinois. Lincoln's supporters wanted only the best railroad car available to carry the casket on the last leg of its journey from Chicago to Springfield. The president's friends chose Pullman's Pioneer. Along the route, the tops of bridges had to be raised and station platforms trimmed to accommodate the huge car. Thousands of people gathered at trackside to watch as the train made its way over the Illinois flatlands with its engine bells tolling a funeral dirge. The people, though deeply saddened by the loss of their leader, could not help being impressed by Pullman's marvelous passenger car.

The Pullman Palace Car Company

By the end of 1867, forty-eight Pullman cars were in service. Also in 1867, George Pullman formally organized the Pullman Palace Car Company. In addition to sleeping cars, the company built "hotel cars," with a kitchen at one end. In the hotel cars, riders sat and ate elegant meals as the miles whizzed by. For the very rich, Pullman made "parlor cars," luxurious coaches that allowed men and women to sit on upholstered chairs as comfortable as the armchairs in their parlors at home. Chairs in the parlor cars were built on swivels so that passengers could turn and face each other while they chatted. Or they could turn the other way and gaze out the window at the scenery. The Pullman name soon became synonymous with the very finest in luxury travel.

Pullman did not sell his cars to the railroads. Instead he leased his equipment, and retained full control of the services offered in the cars. In this way, passengers in sleeping cars were tended by Pullman porters, and customers in dining cars were served dinner by Pullman waiters. Pullman insisted that his employees always wear impeccably clean uniforms and treat customers with dignity. Riders affectionately called porters "Georgies," after the company owner.

Traveling on Pullman cars cost more. A sleeping car ticket for one night usually cost two dollars more than the coach fare charged by railroads. But even middle-class people were glad to pay the extra amount. The fancy coaches were so popular that a passenger often had to order tickets weeks in advance for the privilege of riding in a Pullman car.

Across the nation, railroads expanded as if there were no limits. Between 1850 and 1900, some 190,000 miles of track were built. In 1869, a national dream was realized with the opening of the transcontinental railroad. It was now possible to take a train from New York City all the way to San Francisco. Such a cross-country trip took seven to ten days on the trains of the time. Clearly there was a need for more comfortable sleeping cars.

The Most Perfect City in the World

With a constant demand for new cars, Pullman's factory and offices expanded. In October 1871, the Great Chicago Fire raged through the downtown section. Pullman's offices were reduced to ashes, along with most of the city. But Pullman dismissed the fire as a mere setback in his plans. He had more glorious dreams—the dreams to build an empire.

In the 1870s, Pullman traveled to England where he sold the British railroad system dozens of his luxury cars. No doubt he visited Saltaire, an English industrial village that centered around a woolens factory. Saltaire was one of several experiments in living that took place during the Industrial Revolution. It was a factory town designed to place workers close to the industrial plants, and at the same time, give factory hands decent houses for their families. Pullman liked the idea. And—as was true with his sleeping cars years earlier—he thought he could build an even better industrial village.

Quietly, Pullman bought about three thousand acres of land eleven miles south of Chicago. It was a marshy region on the shores of Lake Calumet. Pullman reasoned that a village built here would take workers away from the grime of the city and put them in a healthy country atmosphere. This setting would bene-fit the workers as well as the Pullman Palace Car Company.

Between 1880 and 1885, Pullman drained the land and built his model town. He hired a talented young architect named Solon Beman to lay out streets and design rows of houses for workers. Beman also drew plans for factory buildings and a grand administration office. He placed these structures in the center of the small city. This was America's first large industrial vil-lage to be planned from the start, and George Pullman insisted that it be perfect in every detail.

Fifteen hundred laborers, most of them hired per-sonally by George Pullman, swarmed over the construction site. The men erected factories, offices, a market, and hundreds of houses. Pullman chose the building materials: common brick for the workers' houses, red brick for central buildings, and an intriguing green stone for the church. Historian Hugh Dalziel

Much of the town was still under construction at the time this photograph of housing in north Pullman was taken in 1885.

Duncan later wrote, "The building of Pullman was one of the great architectural and engineering dramas of Chicago."[5]

When it was completed in 1885, the town held almost nine thousand people, all of them Pullman employees and their families. It was a marvel to behold. The Pullman Palace Car Administration Building, crowned with a tall clock tower, dominated the town. A three-acre lake, whose shores were beautifully landscaped with shrubs and flowers, spread in front of the main building. Prime housing consisted of sturdy red-brick apartment buildings for foremen and company officers. In the center of the housing area stood Market Hall, also called the Arcade. The ground floor of this three-story market building held stores where company employees bought bread, meat, and vegetables. Upper floors housed various businesses, including watchmakers, shoe-repair shops, and doctors' offices. The town astounded visitors with its neatness and architectural grace. In 1885, a reporter for the *Inter Ocean* said, "It [the town] is already famous as one of the wonders of the west. . . . More completely and on a larger scale than was ever before attempted, there is seen here a sympathetic blending of the useful and beautiful."[6]

At George Pullman's insistence, village streets were named for great inventors. These were men, like himself, who became famous on the strength of their ideas. There was a Watt Street, named after James Watt, who developed the steam engine. Fulton Street honored Robert Fulton, who built the world's first commercially successful steamboat. Morse Avenue memorialized Samuel Morse, the inventor of the telegraph. Of course, there was a Pullman Street, and the town itself was called Pullman, Illinois. It was a perfect kingdom for George Pullman, the sleeping car king.

The Life of an Empire Builder

George Pullman did not live in the town he created. His home was a mansion on Prairie Avenue where Chicago's millionaires lived. His neighbors included

This view of the town of Pullman, Illinois, was taken from the roof of the Arcade building.

the Armour family, whose stockyards shipped meat to every city in the nation. Marshal Field, president of one of the world's largest department stores, also lived nearby. Grandest of all the Prairie Street homes was Pullman's, a three-story graystone with extensive private gardens.

A single railroad track led from Pullman's mansion to the town he built eleven miles to the south. Every morning Pullman took a private railroad car to his administration building and began work. In his office, he read sales proposals and participated in staff meetings. At least once a day, he toured the factory buildings to personally inspect the cars as they were being built. Over the years, the company expanded to manufacture freight cars and streetcars for city surface lines. Pullman carefully looked over each vehicle. Paying close attention to details was the key to his success, and

Pullman devoted much of his personal attention to the business he built. Here, he inspects a wheel on a passenger car.

he would not abandon that principle even now when he was one of the country's richest men. As he walked through the factory he had little to say to workers. The managers and office staff regarded him with a combination of respect and trembling fear. One office worker said, "I never knew a man so reserved. He was always mighty good to me, and I think he'd have liked to treat others that way and make them his friends. But he couldn't. He just didn't know how."[7]

Many observers claim his family life, too, was reserved. In 1867, Pullman married Harriet Sager, the daughter of a prominent Chicago railroad contractor. The marriage produced two daughters and twin boys. Harriet was a charming woman who easily mixed in with Chicago's high society. The Pullmans' daughter Harriet, whom the family called "Little Hattie," was bright and lively. George Pullman, however, was disappointed by the free and easy lifestyle enjoyed by his two sons. The boys acted as if the private schools and expensive vacations they enjoyed were their birthright, unquestioned privileges of the rich. Contrasted with Pullman's own impoverished childhood, the Pullman sons were hopelessly spoiled. On the other hand, Pullman adored his other daughter, Florence. Insiders said the only time he ever laughed or smiled at work was when Florence visited the office. A landmark in Pullman, Illinois, was an elegant hotel where guests of the company stayed. It was called the Hotel Florence.

In his leisure hours, Pullman played cards with his neighbor Marshal Field. He threw parties attended by

George Pullman married Harriet Sager in 1867. Although Pullman was reserved in his personal life, the marriage was a happy one that produced four children.

Florence Pullman was George Pullman's favorite daughter and the namesake of the Hotel Florence.

Chicago's rich and powerful. George Pullman's mansion included a pipe organ and a small theater. Like the homes of most of their neighbors on Prairie Avenue, the Pullmans' mansion was packed with paintings and sculptures. Pullman's taste for luxury extended even to his private railroad car. Built especially for him, the car cost more than many fancy homes of the time. Pullman did not favor any political party, but he was always friendly with politicians. Pullman loaned his private car to various presidents, including Benjamin Harrison and Grover Cleveland.

The sleeping car king had achieved success exceeding his dreams. Yet many people claimed that he was without a true friend. He lived harboring suspicions of others. His riches trapped him like a king who feared rivals to his throne. One of his neighbors was overheard to say, "He [Pullman] was one of the most frigid, pompous autocrats [rulers] I have ever seen."[8]

*T*he poor working girl,
May heaven protect her,
She has such an awfully
    hard time;
The rich man's daughter
    goes haughtily by,
My God! do you wonder
    at crime!

—From a ballad called
"The Poor Working Girl,"
sung by factory ladies in
various American cities.[1]

THE GILDED AGE

The Mansion and the Slum

Writer Mark Twain described the Industrial Revolution in nineteenth-century America as the Gilded Age. The word *gilded* means gold-coated. The term described how the upper class lived.

During the Gilded Age, the American rich enjoyed comforts and material abundance exceeding that of European kings and queens. Some millionaires believed, like the royalty of old, that their wealth and power was part of a divine plan. "God gave me my money," said John D. Rockefeller, the richest of the rich Americans.[2]

Life in the Gilded Age

Gilded Age workers, on the other hand, faced lives of insecurity and bewildering change. The reliance on machines to produce goods transformed American workers from craftsmen to units on a production line. Before the Industrial Revolution, a skilled carpenter built a horse-drawn wagon from the wheels up. But during the industrial era, the typical worker operated a machine that produced only the spokes on the wagon wheels. This system lowered the status of the worker, making it more difficult to take individual pride in the result of one's work.

Machines increased production, but their use often depressed wages. It was easier to train a machine operator to do one simple task than it was to teach a craftsman to complete a finished product. Therefore, machine operators were readily replaced and could not demand more money for their labor. An 1884 study conducted by the state of Illinois concluded that the average factory machine operator earned $525 a year. That operator's family had bare minimum annual expenses of $507. This left the family with eighteen dollars a year for any expenses above basic needs. A worker at the Pullman Palace Car Company complained, "When a man is steady and sober and has a saving wife . . . , and after working two and a half years for a company and [still] finds himself in debt for a common living, something must be wrong."[3]

Industrialization also transformed the United States into a nation of cities. In 1840, the vast majority of Americans lived on small farms. Industry was confined to village shops where a blacksmith made horseshoes and a miller ground wheat into meal. Then factories opened in the cities. The number of factory jobs increased five-fold between 1860 and 1900. Men and women who had lived in rural areas for generations uprooted their families, seeking factory employment and the excitement offered by big city life.

The population of the United States doubled between 1870 and 1900. This increase came through natural growth and as a result of immigration. More than a quarter million people a year entered the country in the late 1800s. Most of the newcomers arrived from southern and eastern Europe. Many were Catholic and Jewish. Their customs differed sharply from those of earlier Americans, the bulk of whom came from northern Europe or the British Isles. The new immigrants, bewildered and poor, crowded into the cities and took industrial jobs.

As the cities expanded, their slums festered. Families lived in tenement houses, crowded three or four to a room. A single city block was often home to more than one thousand people, most of them poor. Diseases such as cholera, tuberculosis, and typhoid fever reached epidemic proportions in working-class neighborhoods. Half the babies born in Chicago in 1890 would die before they reached five years of age.

During the Gilded Age, factory workers toiled sixty hours a week for low pay. Child labor was common. Everyone lived in fear of business slumps that struck the national economy with grim regularity. In the grip of such slumps, factories dismissed workers. In those days, an unemployed worker could expect no help

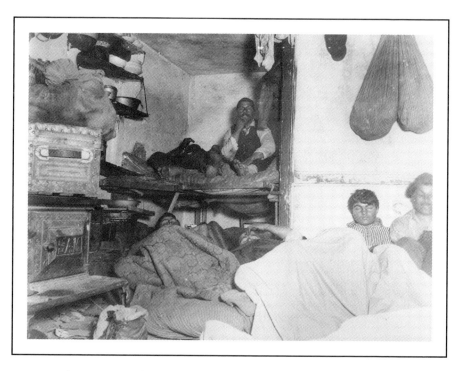

This picture of a slum apartment in New York City was taken in 1890 by famous photographer Jacob Riis.

from the government. Hunger and homelessness were the lot of many big-city workers.

Booming Chicago was the nation's greatest testament to the machine era. The city held sixty-six firms that employed more than five hundred factory hands. Some industries were true giants. On the west side sprawled the McCormick Harvesting Machine plant. Here were assembled reapers and other farm machinery, giant whirling machines that did the work of ten field hands. On the south side stood the city's famous

SOURCE DOCUMENT

AFTER THE FUNERAL . . . I ASKED [THE MOTHER] IF THERE WAS ANYTHING MORE WE COULD DO FOR HER. THE OVER-WORKED, SORROW-STRICKEN WOMAN LOOKED UP AND REPLIED, "I WOULD LIKE NOT TO GO TO WORK IN THE FACTORY [TOMORROW]. I WOULD LIKE TO STAY AT HOME ALL DAY AND HOLD [MY OTHER] BABY. GOOSIE WAS ALWAYS ASKING ME TO HOLD HIM AND I NEVER HAD ANY TIME." THIS STATEMENT REVEALED THE CONDITION OF MANY MOTHERS WHO ARE OBLIGED TO FOREGO THE JOYS AND SOLACES WHICH BELONG TO EVEN THE MOST POVERTY-STRICKEN. THE LONG HOURS OF FACTORY LABOR NECESSARY FOR EARNING THE SUPPORT OF A CHILD LEAVE NO TIME FOR THE TENDER CARE AND CARESSING WHICH MAY ENRICH THE LIFE OF THE MOST PITEOUS [WORTHY OF PITY] BABY.[4]

Jane Addams (1860–1935) was a famous social worker who ran a settlement called Hull House on Halsted Street in the Chicago slums. Addams told this sad story of a factory-working mother whose five-year-old boy, nicknamed Goosie, was killed when he fell off a roof in a tenement house.

stockyards. Here cattle were slaughtered in assembly-line fashion at the rate of a dozen a minute. Chicago's factory network was strung together by railroads. The city was the world's biggest railroad center, with three thousand miles of track and more than one hundred trains arriving and departing daily.

Industrialized Chicago was noisy, smoky, and smelly. A choking stench from the stockyards covered the entire south side. City residents spoke many languages.

The Pullman mansion on Chicago's elite Prairie Avenue is seen here as it looked in the 1880s.

Some 80 percent of Chicagoans were either European immigrants or the children of immigrants. The city's slums were among the worst in the world. Yet along Prairie Avenue rose the mansions of the wealthy—the Armours, the McCormicks, the Fields, and the Pullmans. This contrast between mansion and slum brewed bitter feelings in Chicago during the Gilded Age. Finally, the bitterness boiled over like a pot of stew left too long on the fire.

Class Warfare

Thanksgiving Day, 1884, was supposed to be a time of celebration where families gathered around dinner tables piled high with food. Instead, hundreds of men and women, shouting and cursing, marched down Chicago's Michigan Avenue. The angry parade headed toward the mansions in the Prairie Avenue district.

On this traditional feast day, the marchers carried the black flag, a symbol of hunger. The nation was in the grip of a business slump, a plague that all too frequently haunted industrialized America. More than thirty thousand Chicago workers had lost their jobs. Families of the unemployed suffered from hunger, even on Thanksgiving Day. Upon reaching Prairie Avenue, members of the mob pounded on the doors of the McCormicks, the Armours, the Pullmans, the Fields, and other houses of the well-to-do. No one answered the angry knocks. The rich Chicagoans were locked inside their houses, trying to enjoy their Thanksgiving dinners.

In the late 1800s, the United States suffered through bitter times that threatened to explode into class warfare. The poor hated the rich. The rich regarded the poor as lazy or irresponsible. Capital—the business owners, feuded with labor—the employees. By 1890, some Americans feared a new civil war would break out in the United States. This new civil war would be a bloody conflict between the haves and the have nots, capital against labor. The initial battles in this war of the Gilded Age had already been fought.

In 1877, a strike by railroad workers in West Virginia spread to involve railroad employees in other states. Fistfights and rock-throwing incidents escalated into gun battles between police and strikers. Mobs roamed the streets of Baltimore, Maryland, looting and burning buildings. St. Louis, Missouri, was virtually shut down for five days due to rioting. Around the country some one hundred people were killed, thirty of them in Chicago.

Such class warfare was common in Europe, but it was viewed as a shocking development in the United States. This well-fed nation had never before experienced bread riots. But the lure of city life had pulled people off the farms and made them dependent on factory jobs. Now workers were subject to forces over which they had no control. Rich people had money in banks that allowed them to survive the ups and downs of business cycles. The poor had no such reserves.

Comfortable Americans blamed the hostilities between rich and poor on the thousands of immigrants flooding into the country in recent years. The Irish were known to form unions and become labor rousers. Some of the worst troublemakers were the Germans. In 1848, Germany was rocked by a series of rebellions among industrial and farm workers. A dictatorship then took over in Germany and jailed or executed the rebels. Thousands of German rebels fled their old country and settled in United States cities. The population of Chicago was almost one quarter German-born by the end of the nineteenth century. Between 1870 and 1880, not one year passed without a major strike paralyzing the city. Most of these strikes were led by German unionists.

The Haymarket Massacre

One of the bloodiest years in the nineteenth-century labor wars came in 1886. Some fifteen hundred strikes, big and small, broke out around the country. The most explosive issue was labor's call for the eight-hour day. At the time, factory hands regularly toiled through exhausting ten- or even twelve-hour shifts. Enough! cried labor. Unions came up with a motto that members chanted as if it were a cheer at a football game:

> *Eight hours for work.*
> *Eight hours for recreation, Rest.*
> *Eight hours for sleep.*[5]

Capital believed the eight-hour workday would cut into their profits. Thus the lines for class warfare were drawn in deadly fashion. Labor leaders called for a national strike to take place on May 1—May Day—1886. On May Day, no worker was to report to his or her job. Tension gripped the nation as many expected violence in front of factory entrances.

May Day, 1886, came and went without incident. Sporadic strikes took place, but there was no nationwide walkout as envisioned by labor leaders. On May 3, however, a fight broke out between strikers and non-strikers at Chicago's McCormick Harvesting Machine works. Security guards waded into the mob, clubbing heads and firing pistols. Screams, curses, and the sickening thud of clubs crashing on skulls filled the air. The ghastly scene infuriated German-born labor leader August Spies. He called for a mass meeting to take place the next day at Chicago's Haymarket Square, just

WE MEAN TO MAKE THINGS OVER, WE ARE TIRED OF TOIL FOR NAUGHT,

WITH BUT BARE ENOUGH TO LIVE UPON, AND NE'ER AN HOUR FOR THOUGHT;

WE WANT TO FEEL THE SUNSHINE, AND WE WANT TO SMELL THE FLOWERS,

WE ARE SURE THAT GOD HAS WILLED IT, AND WE MEAN TO HAVE EIGHT HOURS.

WE'RE SUMMONING OUR FORCES FROM THE SHIPYARD, SHOP, AND MILL.

CHORUS:

EIGHT HOURS FOR WORK, EIGHT HOURS FOR REST, EIGHT HOURS FOR WHAT WE WILL.

EIGHT HOURS FOR WORK, EIGHT HOURS FOR REST, EIGHT HOURS FOR WHAT WE WILL.

THE BEASTS THAT GRAZE THE HILLSIDE, AND THE BIRDS THAT WANDER FREE,

IN THE LIFE THAT GOD HAS METED, HAVE A BETTER LOT THAN WE.

OH HANDS AND HEARTS ARE WEARY, AND HOMES ARE HEAVY WITH DOLE.

IF OUR LIFE'S TO BE FILLED WITH DRUDGERY, WHAT NEED OF A HUMAN SOUL?

SHOUT, SHOUT THE LUSTY RALLY, FROM SHIPYARD, SHOP, AND MILL.[6]

Workers raised their spirits by shouting slogans and singing songs. This song, called "Eight Hour Day," was sung by striking workers at Chicago's McCormick Harvesting Machine plant in 1886, on the eve of the Haymarket Massacre.

west of downtown. Printing presses churned out handbills, which were given to workers: "Revenge! Workingmen! To Arms!"[7]

Police stood guard everywhere on the night of May 4, 1886. Rich Chicagoans shuddered in fear. The wealthy regarded August Spies and the others calling for the protest meeting as the most dangerous of the city's labor leaders. Spies and his followers were anarchists, a small core of radicals who rejected all forms of government. The anarchists spread fear among many Americans, even though they were never a powerful force in the country. Terrorism against the state and outright warfare against the police were common tactics among anarchists.

The nighttime meeting at Haymarket Square began peacefully. People made fiery speeches. The working-class audience shouted out curses. But there was no violence. Rain began to fall, and many in the crowd started for home.

Then a stick-like object, sparkling in the night, bounced in front of the ranks of policemen. A terrible explosion, which flashed like a blinding lightning bolt and burst with a powerful thunder clap, ripped through Haymarket Square. Someone had thrown a dynamite bomb into the crowd. Police opened fire, and for a nightmarish two minutes, bullets whizzed in every direction. People screamed and stumbled over each other, seeking cover. When some sense of order returned to Haymarket Square, authorities counted casualties. Eight police officers and two members of the crowd were killed. Many of the dead—police and civilians—were victims of the wild crossfire. Some sixty persons were injured.

Newspapers called the bombing the "Haymarket Massacre." Stories in the press claimed it was the worst of all battles in the labor war then raging in the United States. "Now It Is Blood," blared one Chicago headline the next morning.[8]

Eight anarchists were arrested and brought to trial. It was never determined who threw the bomb. The court sentenced seven labor leaders to death by hanging and one to a fifteen-year prison term. This sentence came despite the fact that only two of the defendants were even present at Haymarket Square on the night of the bombing. Four men, including August Spies, were hanged. Another committed suicide in his jail cell, and the rest were eventually released.

Like no other incident, the Haymarket Massacre shook the lives of well-to-do Chicagoans. Because of the clash, the rich of Prairie Avenue moved to suburbs such as Wilmette and Glencoe along the northern shore of Lake Michigan. Chicago, they reasoned, was finished as a major city, since it was full of hate-filled European radicals led by lawless anarchists. The wealthy used their influence in Washington, D.C., and persuaded the government to build an army base, Fort Sheridan, along the lake shore. Fort Sheridan had no purpose other than to protect nearby families and to send troops to Chicago if needed to put down riots in that hotbed of revolution.

SOURCE DOCUMENT

IF YOU THINK BY HANGING US YOU CAN STAMP OUT THE LABOR MOVEMENT . . . THE MOVEMENT FROM WHICH THE DOWN-TRODDEN MILLIONS, THE MILLIONS WHO TOIL IN WANT AND MISERY, EXPECT SALVATION, IF THIS IS YOUR OPINION, THEN HANG US! [BUT] BEHIND YOU AND IN FRONT OF YOU, AND EVERYWHERE FLAMES BLAZE UP. IT IS A SUBTERRANEAN [BENEATH THE SURFACE] FIRE. YOU CANNOT PUT IT OUT.[9]

The defiance and the bitterness as well as the bravery of Gilded Age labor leaders can be seen in this statement by August Spies shortly before he was hanged for his alleged involvement in the Haymarket Massacre.

Over the next few decades, the bloodshed at Haymarket Square faded in American memory, but it had a lasting effect overseas. The grossly unfair trial of the Haymarket leaders became a rallying cry for Europe's budding Communist movement. The Communists believed in state ownership of factories and farms. In twentieth-century Communist countries, May Day—the call for the eight-hour day—became the cause for a great patriotic holiday. The Soviet Union reserved May Day, May 1, for gigantic parades to celebrate communism. Speakers at Communist May Day gatherings extolled the courage shown by "the heroes of Chicago."

*When the unions'
inspiration through
the workers' blood shall
run.*

*There can be no power
greater anywhere
beneath the sun.*

*Yet what force on earth
is weaker than the fee-
ble strength of one?*

*But the union makes us
strong!*

Chorus:

*Solidarity forever, Solidarity forever, Solidarity forever,
For the union makes us strong!*

4

SOLIDARITY FOREVER

—A rallying song written in the Gilded Age by union organizer
Ralph Chaplin. The song was sung to the tune of "Battle Hymn of
the Republic," and its message urged workers to overcome their
fears and stick together despite all hazards.[1]

The Unions

People in the industrial era could refuse to work for unfair wages. But factory owners viewed workers as parts of a machine that could always be replaced. Therefore, to demand better wages, workers had to stick together and withhold their labor collectively in the form of a strike. The need for workers to act as a large group led to the growth of unions.

The first important nationwide union was the Knights of Labor, organized by garment workers in

Philadelphia in 1869. More than just a labor union, the Knights were a political movement. Membership was open to farmers, merchants, even doctors—anyone who was sympathetic to the cause of labor. Among the organization's goals were the abolition of child labor and the establishment of the eight-hour workday. Under the leadership of Terence V. Powderly, the Knights of Labor won a major railroad strike in 1885. A year later, the organization had grown to seven hundred thousand members. But a crushing defeat in a second railroad strike deflated the union's power. By 1900, the group was a memory. Still, for many years after the union's demise, old-timers sang its rousing song:

> *Storm the fort, ye*
> *Knights of Labor*
> *Battle for your cause:*
> *Equal rights for every neighbor*
> *Down with Tyrant laws.*[2]

In contrast to the Knights, another union called the American Federation of Labor (AFL) concentrated on bread-and-butter issues important to working people. Established in the 1880s, the AFL was open only to wage earners. This excluded farmers, shopkeepers, and owners of small businesses. The organization shunned politics and proposed no grand social schemes. Its official motto was simple: "A fair day's wage for a fair day's work."[3] The AFL would strike if it believed a strike was necessary, but first the union sought to bargain with employers to achieve its goals.

The AFL's leader throughout its early years was the remarkable Samuel Gompers (1850–1924). Born in England, Gompers came to the United States at age thirteen. He lived in New York City and became, like his father, a cigarmaker. In those days, cigarmakers sat together in crowded shops rolling cigars on benches. To fight boredom, they chipped in a few pennies to pay someone to read to them while they worked. Gompers had no formal education, but the cigar shop readings excited his desire to learn. He studied history and developed his own ideas on unionism. Gompers organized a cigarmakers' union, and then graduated to leadership in the AFL. Under his direction, the AFL became the nation's most successful labor union.

Some unions in the Gilded Age were devoted to violence and preached revolution against the rich. One such organization was a semi-secret society of coal miners called the Molly Maguires. Coal mining was a harsh life. Men and boys worked side-by-side in dark mines, often knee-deep in water, and always facing the dangers of an explosion or a cave-in. Coal mining strikes were usually bloody affairs. Made up largely of Irishmen, the Molly Maguires issued threats to kill mine owners and to beat up fellow miners who refused to join labor strikes. It was never clear to what extent the Molly Maguires acted on their threats, but mainstream America looked upon the militant miners with dread. A labor leader accused of being a "Molly" was likely to be arrested, imprisoned, and sometimes executed.

SOURCE DOCUMENT

I MAINTAIN THAT THE HOURS OF LABOR OUGHT TO BE REDUCED. FROM EVERY STANDPOINT THE HOURS ARE TOO LONG IN MODERN INDUSTRIES . . . WHERE THE INDIVIDUAL, THE WORKER, IS BUT A PART OF A MACHINE AND IS COMPELLED TO KEEP IN MOTION IN ACCORDANCE WITH THE VELOCITY [SPEED] WITH WHICH THE MACHINE TURNS. . . . THE REDUCTION OF THE HOURS OF LABOR REACHES THE VERY ROOT OF SOCIETY. IT GIVES THE WORKINGMAN BETTER CONDITIONS AND BETTER OPPORTUNITIES, AND MAKES OF HIM WHAT HAS BEEN TOO LONG NEGLECTED—A CONSUMER INSTEAD OF A MERE PRODUCER.[4]

In the late nineteenth century, factory hands worked ten hours a day and six days a week. It was not until the 1920s that the eight-hour day became common. Finally, in the 1930s, the eight-hour day, five-day week (forty-hour week) became the law of the land. These are the words of labor leader Samuel Gompers, speaking in favor of the eight-hour day before the United States Senate in 1885.

Union Busting

Owners of large industries fought the union movement. Factories cooperated with each other by exchanging blacklists, lists containing the names of workers known to be union organizers. Anyone whose name appeared on the blacklist was denied a job. Businesses pressured state governments to pass laws restricting union activities. Captains of industry—the owners of large businesses—also had influence over the press. Newspapers commonly played on fears that the unions had been taken over by anarchists who sought the destruction of law and order. The United States at the time had a growing and very comfortable middle class. Many middle-class Americans worried that political power would pass to members of the working class, who were poorly educated, crude, prone to violence, and increasingly foreign in their make-up.

Most businesses pursued a policy of union-busting in the late 1800s. Often, however, it required very little push from big business to upset a union's structure. Working people were divided between the skilled and the unskilled, black and white, male and female, and English-speaking and foreign members. Constant bickering caused many labor unions to self-destruct.

Friction between skilled and unskilled workers was a never-ending problem for unions. The railroads, for example, employed highly trained mechanics and engineers as well as people whose only job was to shovel coal. The skilled employees enjoyed higher pay and greater benefits than did the coal shovelers. Skilled men jealously guarded their privileges and cared little about the working conditions faced by laborers. Therefore, it was difficult to organize one industry-wide railroad union. Instead craft unions such as the engineers or the mechanics prevailed in the railroad industry.

Racial and ethnic hatreds were an even more serious problem for unions. In the late 1800s, the vast majority of blacks lived in the South, where they worked on farms. As African Americans began moving north and taking industrial jobs, white workers resented their competition. Some factory owners promoted racial hatreds by hiring blacks as strike-breakers. Divisions between English-speaking Americans and the foreign-born also upset unions. Long-standing Americans complained that immigrants from Europe were too willing to accept low pay and harsh working conditions. Therefore, the foreigners were stealing American jobs.

Women entering the workplace presented another problem. In the past, women were expected to stay home and tend to the house and children while men worked. The rise of factories changed women's traditional roles. Factories—especially those that produced clothes—required low-paid people to cut and sew cloth. As a result, masses of women took factory jobs. In the nineteenth century, no laws guaranteed equal rights to women workers. Women were usually restricted to sewing clothes in cramped, airless factories called "sweatshops." Few industrial unions accepted women. When women were allowed to organize, they became some of the most spirited unionists in the country. But they could not draw men into their fold. Workingmen regarded "women's work" as chores that were beneath them, and they refused to join ranks with female workers.

"Solidarity Forever," said the popular union rallying song. But working people fought each other often more vigorously than they opposed the bosses. Capitalists knew the ranks of labor were deeply divided and exploited this weakness whenever possible. Jay Gould, the millionaire railroad owner, once said, "I can hire one half the working class to kill the other half."[5]

Eugene V. Debs and His Dream

James Whitcomb Riley was a poet, born in Indiana in 1849. He wrote about farmers, storekeepers, and other working people. One of Riley's greatest heroes was labor leader Eugene Debs. Of Debs he wrote:

> *And there's 'Gene Debs—a man 'at stands*
> *And just holds out in his two hands*
> *As warm a heart as ever beat*
> *Betwixt here and the Jedgement seat!*[6]

Debs inspired poetry because he possessed a rare trait—he was a totally unselfish man. He sought to better the lives of working people while caring little about personal gains.

Eugene Victor Debs was born in Terre Haute, Indiana, in 1855. His father came from a prosperous and educated family in France, but he lost contact with his family when he immigrated to the United States. In the new country, the elder Debs took jobs as a railroad laborer and as a meat packer in a slaughterhouse. The family's real source of income was a grocery store that Marguerite Debs, Eugene's mother, ran from the parlor of her modest house. The father was a dreamer, devoted to books and to art. The mother was a practical

Eugene Debs, whose modest background was similar to Pullman's own, is seen at about the time of the Pullman strike.

businesswoman who largely supported the family of six children. Eugene Debs inherited the abilities and aspirations of both parents.

At age fourteen, Debs quit school and took a job to help support the family. For fifty cents a day he scraped paint off the sides of old freight cars at the Terre Haute railroad yard. One night, the fireman assigned to a train engine got drunk and failed to report to his job. The engineer picked young Eugene Debs to shovel coal into the firebox and tend to the boiler. Thus the teenage Debs landed a steady job as a fireman on the Terre Haute and Indianapolis Railroad. His pay was now a dollar a day.

Like his father, Eugene Debs had a hunger for reading. He bought an encyclopedia, and quickly read through all ten volumes. History, economics, politics, and philosophy interested him most. His favorite novel was *Les Misérables* by French author Victor Hugo. The book told the story of a poor man who stole a loaf of bread to feed his family and spent nineteen years in prison as punishment for the crime. Debs reread the book many times, quoted passages of it line for line, and often spoke of the injustice suffered by the novel's main character, Jean Valjean.

Working on trains furthered Debs's education. As a fireman in the engine compartment, he traveled through prosperous communities as well as wretched slums. In hard times he saw hungry families share their food with neighbors who were near starvation. One night, Debs lost a close friend, an overworked young man who slipped on the tracks and was cut in half under the wheels of a freight train. He later wrote,

> As a locomotive fireman I learned of the hardships of the rail in snow, sleet, and hail, of the ceaseless danger that lurks along the iron highway, the uncertainty of employment, scant wages and altogether trying lot of the workingman, so that from my very boyhood I was made to feel the wrongs of labor.[7]

At an early age, Debs concluded that working people could better their lot only with the help of labor unions. He joined the Brotherhood of Locomotive Firemen and soon became a union officer. Although he had little formal education, Debs also served on the town library board and led a literary discussion group. He was elected city clerk of Terre Haute. Voters later sent him to the Indiana legislature. Debs married Katherine Metzel at age thirty. He was by all measures a respected man in the Terre Haute community. Wealthy townspeople, however, worried about his extreme views when he talked about labor unions and the rights of working people.

As was true with George Pullman, Debs nurtured a single idea. He wanted to organize all railroad workers into a single union. It did little good for his own union, the Locomotive Firemen, to go on strike when other workers, such as the switchmen or the brakemen, stayed on the job. A strong railroad union had to include all workers, united in a single cause. To form an industrywide union he would have to persuade skilled men to give up the loyalties they held to their trade organizations. This was a difficult task, because old loyalties die hard. But Eugene Debs had developed into an excellent writer and a brilliant speaker. Fully devoted to the dream of forming a national railroad union, he was a very persuasive young man.

In 1893, Debs organized the American Railway Union (ARU). True to his dream, the ARU embraced all railroad trades—the switchmen, brakemen, firemen, engineers, and unskilled workers. However, the new union rejected African Americans. Debs was furious with this development. He had hoped his union would welcome black workers. Resistance came from men who refused to work side-by-side with Negroes, as African Americans were called at that time. Debs could not risk breaking up his organization over the anti-black

SOURCE DOCUMENT

FOR THE PURPOSES OF [OUR] PROTECTION, THE THROTTLE AND THE SCOOP, THE SWITCH AND THE BRAKE, MUST BE IN CLOSE ALLIANCE, AND EQUALLY FIRM AND DEFIANT, AND WHEN CORPORATIONS SEE THIS FEDERATION ACCOMPLISHED, NO STRIKES WILL OCCUR, BECAUSE A STRIKE UNDER SUCH CIRCUMSTANCES WOULD MEAN AN IMMEDIATE CESSATION OF RAILROAD TRANSPORTATION ON THE LINE OR SYSTEM WHERE IT OCCURRED.[8]

As an officer in the Brotherhood of Locomotive Firemen, Debs often lectured other members on the need to broaden their union. This is an excerpt from a speech he made to his union in 1886.

measures. So he swallowed his anger and forged ahead, leading his new union.

Just months after the ARU was born, James J. Hill, the owner of the Great Northern Railroad, cut the pay for common workers from $1.25 a day to $1.00 a day. This reduction affected unskilled men only. Normally, those laborers would have to shrug their shoulders and accept their loss. They knew that any strike on their part, without the help of the skilled trades, was bound to lose. But workers on the Great Northern Railroad had been organized by the ARU. Now, when the unskilled hands walked off their jobs, all others walked with them. This collective action shut down the Great Northern Railroad for more than two weeks. Hill, furious over this development, restored the unskilled workers' pay.

The ARU had won an important victory over James J. Hill and his railroad. Soon the young union faced a far more difficult and dangerous clash—the Pullman strike.

We are born in a Pullman house, fed from the Pullman shop, taught in the Pullman school, catechized in the Pullman church, and when we die we shall be buried in the Pullman cemetery and go to the Pullman hell.

—An unnamed employee of the Pullman Palace Car Company.[1]

TROUBLE IN PARADISE

A Utopia Gone Wrong

The word *utopia* comes from a book written in 1516 by the English scholar Thomas More. It describes an imaginary land where everything was perfect. Some writers in the late nineteenth century compared Pullman, Illinois, to the mythical Utopia. On the surface, the town seemed to have reached perfection. It was neat, it was orderly, and the streets were clean. One man in the 1890s came to Pullman on the local railroad and exclaimed, "I stepped from the cars. Beauty, grace and art met me on every hand. . . . Eye and taste were at once content and glad."[2] Town residents enjoyed a youth baseball team, an eighty-piece band that gave concerts in the summer, a community theater that held a thousand people, and a library. Who could fail to be happy in this ideal setting?

The town of Pullman, Illinois, created as an ideal community for workers, is seen here as it looked in pleasant times before the strike.

But most visitors to the town saw only its showcase center—the Hotel Florence, the Arcade, and the housing for managers. In fact, the town's grandest buildings were neatly angled to be seen by passengers riding the Illinois Central Railroad. Few people saw the village outskirts, where the workers lived. One section there had more than one hundred wooden shacks, each one slightly bigger than a modern one-car garage. These frame shanties were unpainted and most had leaky roofs. Brick cottages built for workers were large and

The town of Pullman boasted its own cultural and entertainment activities. The all-boy baseball team of the town of Pullman is seen here.

comfortable, but they all looked just the same. The cottages were also crowded. They had upstairs and downstairs apartments but no private stairways. The family that lived upstairs had to pass through the downstairs dwellers' parlor. Pullman authorities boasted that all cottages had indoor plumbing, a great improvement over most working-class houses in the era. However, two families in each house shared a single faucet and a single toilet. In all the workers' houses there was not one bathtub.

Every foot of ground, each house, every store, even the church was owned by Pullman. Nothing in the town came cheap. The rents and fees added to the company's profits. Rent for the average cottage was 25 to 30 percent higher than a comparable rent in Chicago. The tiny wooden houses cost less than one hundred dollars each to build, yet Pullman charged tenants eight dollars a month. That way, the Pullman Company made back its investment on the houses in a little over a year. Pullman bought water from the city of Chicago. Then he more than doubled the price and resold the water to Pullman residents. The town's handsome Greenstone Church charged pastors a fee to preach there. The fee was so high that there were

SOURCE DOCUMENT

EMPLOYEES . . . WERE TOLD THAT THEIR INTERESTS AND PULLMAN'S WERE ONE AND THE SAME; THAT WHAT WOULD BRING HIM GREATER PROSPERITY WOULD REDOUND [BE] TO THEIR ADVANTAGE. THEY WERE WARNED THAT TO BELONG TO A TRADE UNION WOULD BE INIMICAL [HARMFUL] TO THEIR JOINT ENTERPRISE; AND HENCE ANY WHO JOINED A UNION AMONG THEM WAS TO BE DISCHARGED—REGARDED AS A COMMON ENEMY, AND DRIVEN OUT OF TOWN. HIS PEOPLE WERE TO DEPEND ON HIS GENEROSITY AND FORESIGHT IN ALL THINGS. . . .[3]

The old family saying "father knows best" applied to Pullman, Illinois, where George Pullman was the "father" of all. Journalist John Swinton wrote this account of the model town.

often no Sunday services. Said a newspaper called *The Call*, "He [Pullman] wasn't a man to let you pray for free."[4]

George Pullman controlled all aspects of town life. He once saw a worker discard a piece of paper on the sidewalk and fired the man on the spot. Pullman believed his employees were his children. He and he alone knew what was best for them. Public speakers were not permitted anywhere in the town. Pullman personally censored the plays presented at the town's theater. He excluded any play that might get people angry at authority. He allowed no saloons for the

The Pullman Band, seen in an 1887 photo, was made up of Pullman employees who gave free concerts for other town residents.

workers' use. The fancy Hotel Florence had a bar that served drinks, but it was reserved for rich guests only.

Perhaps the worst aspect of Pullman was the feeling of fear that hung over the town like a cloud. The company employed spies to mingle with the workers and take note of any "troublemaker" who complained about a boss or encouraged others to join a union. Anyone who even talked about unions was reported to company authorities by spies and informers. A reporter named Richard Ely spent ten days in Pullman. He found that people refused to speak with him because

SOURCE DOCUMENT

THERE ARE VARIETY AND FREEDOM ON THE OUTSIDE. THERE ARE MONOTONY AND SURVEILLANCE ON THE INSIDE. NONE OF THE "SUPERIOR" OR "SCIENTIFIC" ADVANTAGES OF THE MODEL CITY WILL COMPENSATE FOR THE RESTRICTIONS ON THE FREEDOM OF THE WORKMEN . . . AND THE CHARGES OF THE COMPANY FOR RENT, HEAT, GAS, WATER [THAT] ARE EXCESSIVE—IF NOT EXTORTIONATE [A CRIMINAL MEANS OF OBTAINING MONEY]. . . . PULLMAN MAY APPEAR TO BE ALL GLITTER AND GLOW, ALL GLADNESS AND GLORY TO THE CASUAL VISITOR, BUT THERE IS THE DEEP, DARK BACKGROUND OF DISCONTENT WHICH IT WOULD BE IDLE TO DENY.[5]

The Chicago Tribune, *the city's biggest newspaper, was a strong supporter of George Pullman and his company. But even the* Tribune *admitted that there were many things amiss in the so-called model town. This story appeared in the paper in 1888.*

they feared he was a spy. Ely concluded, "Here is a population of eight thousand souls where not a single resident dare speak his opinion about the town in which he lives. One feels that one is mingling with a dependent, servile people."[6]

George Pullman learned the lessons of the labor wars of 1877 and the Haymarket Massacre of 1886. Pullman believed the nation's cities, Chicago in particular, were swarming with radicals whose sole purpose was to stir up anger in workers' hearts. His industrial village in the country, he hoped, would shield his workers from the evil influence of the radicals.

Glory and Panic

In 1893, Chicago hosted the World's Fair, an international exhibition designed to show off the latest goods and the modern miracles of science. The Chicago fair was the biggest, most expensive such extravaganza ever held. More than 27 million people came to see the attractions in a wonderland created near the city's lakefront. Guests swooned as they rode the passenger wheel designed by G. W. Ferris, which lifted them two hundred fifty feet into the sky. Electric lighting was a new and fantastic development of the times. Spectators gasped at the Electricity Building, which cast a heavenly glow from the light of a thousand bulbs.

The Pullman Company displayed one of its most luxurious passenger cars at the Transportation Building. There was also a plaster of Paris miniature model of the town George Pullman had created. Many

The Chicago World's Fair, which opened in 1893, was the backdrop of the Pullman strike. Celebrating progress in science and technology, it was a dramatic contrast to the brutal conflict between Pullman and his workers.

fairgoers took a special train to tour the actual village. Of course, they were shown only the center of town and the best of the workers' housing. The tourists were also given a strikingly illustrated pamphlet called *The Story of Pullman*. It said, "Imagine a perfectly equipped town of twelve thousand inhabitants, built from one central thought to a beautiful and harmonious whole. . . . [A town] where all that is ugly and discordant and demoralizing is eliminated."[7]

Chicago's 1893 fair was called the World's Columbian Exposition. It celebrated the four-hundredth anniversary of Christopher Columbus's voyage of discovery. It was also a showcase of American progress during the machine era. A leading journalist said the fair was "the greatest event in the history of the country since the Civil War."[8] But shortly after the fair opened, the country slipped into an economic depression called the Panic of 1893. Around the nation, twelve thousand businesses closed, five hundred banks failed, and as many as 3 million men and women lost their jobs.

Desperate people blamed the rich and the government for their plight. This time, their anger could not be controlled. Just two years earlier, a bloody steel strike in Homestead, Pennsylvania, had cost the lives of thirteen men as workers clashed with police. In May 1893, a ragtag group of jobless men led by a tough scrap-iron dealer named Jacob Coxey marched on Washington, D.C., to demand relief for the impoverished. The group was called Coxey's Army, and many Americans feared the marching men would trigger revolution. Upheaval was in the air. Comfortable Americans trembled when they thought of furious workers taking to the streets armed with clubs, knives, and dynamite.

Chicago held masses of fuming poor people. The city attracted temporary and casual laborers to help build exhibits for the fair. Now more than one hundred thousand homeless and unemployed men roamed the streets. "What a spectacle!" wrote one journalist who visited Chicago during the depression. "What a human downfall after the magnificence of the World's Fair. . . . Heights of splendor in one month: depths of wretchedness, suffering, hunger, cold, in the next."[9]

Despair in Paradise

The depression sharply lowered demand for sleeping cars. Pullman, to his credit, took many orders at a loss to keep workers on the job. But he also slashed the wages of his factory workers by as much as 25 percent. He did this, however, without lowering the rent workers had to pay. Pullman explained that his land-holding company, which owned the town's housing,

These Pullman employees were photographed in 1893, just before the strike.

was a separate organization from his manufacturing company, which produced railroad cars. Therefore, he could not reduce rents because such a reduction would not be fair to the land company. He failed to point out that he—George Pullman—was the main owner of both companies.

There was no iron-clad requirement that a worker had to live in company housing in order to be a company employee. But when business slowed and workers were discharged, the out-of-town employees were first to go. So those Pullman workers who lived in company housing kept their jobs, but they had no choice other than paying high rents with reduced wages.

It was company policy to deduct rent from workers' paychecks. Lowered wages minus the unchanged charges for rent resulted in paychecks that were meager to the point of being cruel. One skilled machinist expected a paycheck of $9.07 for a week's work. When nine dollars was subtracted for rent, he got only seven cents. Thomas Heathcoate, a long-standing employee, said, "I have seen men with families of eight or nine children to support crying because they got only three or four cents after paying their rent; I have seen them stand by the pay window and cry for enough money to keep their families."[10] One man received a check for a penny on payday. He did not cash the check. Instead, he put it in a frame and hung it on his parlor wall to show others the rewards of working for the Pullman Company.

The Pullman Palace Car Company announced wage cuts of 25 percent, but in many departments the reductions were much higher. The company began a stepped-up piecework system that effectively cut pay. Men and women doing piecework were paid by the number of parts or pieces they produced rather than receiving a consistent daily wage. A local minister, the Reverend William Carwardine, worked closely with Pullman employees. He gave this report about how the piecework system slashed wages in the factory.

Despite the depression, the company made money. Pullman stock owners received dividends (money paid to stockholders out of a company's profits) totaling 8 percent on their shares. Why, the workers asked, should they bear the full burden of suffering during these hard times? Surely the company's shareholders could take a cut in dividends as long as employees had to see their wages drastically reduced.

Who were these workers who lived in Pullman housing and built the finest passenger cars on Earth? In 1892, the Pullman Palace Car Company had a

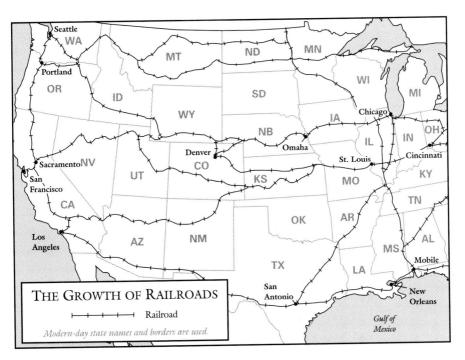

THE GROWTH OF RAILROADS

├──┼──┼──┤ Railroad

Modern-day state names and borders are used.

Through the nineteenth century, railroads expanded across the West. This reliance upon railroads would dramatically increase the effects of the Pullman strike.

payroll of almost six thousand men and women. This workforce would soon be slashed in half due to the hard times of 1893. Reflecting the population of Chicago, about half the workers were foreign-born. Pullman preferred to hire men from Scandinavia and some German immigrants. He feared German radicals, but needed German workmanship. It was rumored that George Pullman distrusted the Irish because they were too close to the politicians who ran Chicago's City Hall. Only about four hundred Pullman workers were Irish. African Americans were not employed at the Pullman factory. White workers would have resisted competition from African Americans, and the company wanted no racial troubles. At the time, most other American factories discriminated against African Americans. However, George Pullman regularly hired African Americans to work as porters on his sleeping cars and dining cars.

The vast majority of Pullman employees were skilled men and women who had served long apprenticeships and were masters of their trades. Pullman Palace Cars remained just that—palaces on wheels. An article in an 1887 newspaper said, "An ordinary passenger [in a Pullman car] travels in as princely a style as any crowned head in Europe."[12] Only professional hands could build these palaces. The inside walls of the cars were lined with polished wood paneling, produced and installed by fine woodworkers. Expert seamstresses sewed padding and fabric to make comfortable seats. More than half the employees were machinists who

Many Pullman residents claimed they could not use the library, seen here, because of the high fees it charged.

produced the wheels, springs, and heavy frames that gave passengers a comfortable ride. These craftspeople were among the finest in the country. Now they were working every day, but earning near starvation wages.

Stories of the sufferings at Pullman were read throughout the United States. A newspaper called the *Chicago Mail* ran a story entitled, "Grim Want in the Model Town."[13] The article began with the word "Starvation," and had the capital *S* of that word held by the figure of a skeleton. Such stories disturbed even high-powered business executives. One such business-man was Cleveland millionaire and factory owner Marcus Hanna. Though he was generally anti-labor, Hanna said of George Pullman, "A man who won't meet his men half-way is a God-damned fool."[14]

The people of Pullman are destitute and starving. Over five thousand human beings are in dire necessity, and appeal to the liberal minded people of Chicago for help. Their unfortunate condition is due to no fault of theirs. They have been noted for their thrift, sobriety, and industry. The fault lies in the hard times and a hard taskmaster. . . .

THE WALKOUT

—An appeal written by the people of Pullman, asking Chicagoans for food and clothing during their time of need.[1]

Winter in Pullman, Illinois

The troubling situation in Pullman, Illinois, captured the country's attention like a great drama taking place on stage. The first act of that drama opened in the winter of 1893 to 1894. Chicago winters can be cruel. Snow covers the ground, and biting winds howl over the flat plains toward the lake. Many Chicagoans claimed the winter of 1893 was the worst in memory. For the people of Pullman, it was the worst of a lifetime.

Pullman workers' cottages were heated by tiny coal stoves. Tenants were required to buy their own coal. That winter, food was scarce, and coal was a luxury few could afford. Cottages grew so cold that water left in a basin overnight froze solid. Few children had proper shoes and coats to wear on the walk to school. Often parents kept children home, bundled in bed all day to protect them from the intense cold.

Work continued in the factory, but layoffs increased in spite of reduced wages. By the spring of 1894, the payroll was reduced to some thirty-five hundred workers, a little more than half the number from three years earlier. Men and women who had been with the company since its beginning were discharged without warning. Thirty years of loyal service meant little to company management. No one who was discharged

Shantytowns grew in Chicago during the Depression of 1893. This one stood near the village of Pullman.

received a pension or any other form of compensation. Pullman bosses and office staff were not let go because they would be hard to replace. Workers, on the other hand, could be rehired when times got better.

Still, some employees chose to stay loyal to George Pullman and his company. The town divided into two camps: the pro- and the anti-Pullman people. Each group adopted its own insignia. The pro-Pullman faction, which included the managers and a small group of factory hands, walked about with an American flag pinned to their shirts. The anti-Pullman people wore a white ribbon on their wrists. In the town the flag and the ribbon stood as opposing banners as if on a battlefield.

The warring factions even divided along spiritual lines. Reverend E. C. Oggel preached at the town's Greenstone Church, and supported George Pullman and his company. "Surely it would seem as if Mr. Pullman has done his part," said Oggel. He described Pullman as a man "who has the noblest ideas and the highest aspirations."[2] On the other hand, Reverend William Carwardine of the First Methodist Episcopal Church denounced company policies. Carwardine ran one of many small church groups that met in and around the town of Pullman. Company officials were unable to control these small congregations, and preachers said what they wished. Carwardine said, "As pastor I came in contact directly with much suffering. Repeated cutting of wages with no corresponding reduction of rent exasperated the employees."[3]

Spring lifted the workers' spirits. But wages remained at their depressed levels and rents were unchanged. Workers were deeply in debt to local grocery stores and just about any other shop that would grant them credit. The spring ushered in the time for determined action.

The Walkout

Meeting in secret, the workers chose a committee of forty-six people to speak for them. Their requests were simple. They wanted wages restored to the level of the previous year, or, if that were impossible, they wanted a reduction in rents. Bearing these demands the committee members walked, unannounced, into the Pullman corporate offices. Company managers were shocked to see a large group of determined-looking union people file through their doors. Still, management agreed to talk.

Meetings were held on May 7 and again on May 9, 1894. George Pullman attended the second meeting. He repeated his argument that wages and rents were not to be mixed because they were handled by separate corporations. The workers were not satisfied with the progress of the talks. But they thought that management had at least agreed not to punish any of the leaders of their small company union.

On the morning of May 10, the Pullman men and women reported to their factory buildings as usual. At the gates, supervisors stopped three men who worked in the Iron Department and told them to go home.

They were fired with no explanation. All three were committee members and vocal supporters of the union. This firing came despite management's supposed promise not to discipline union leaders. An emergency meeting was held that night. Arguments were heard and votes taken. The committee agreed it had no choice but to call for a strike.

The next day, May 11, 1894, Pullman employees reported to work, but everyone talked in whispers. The previous night, union leaders had informed the people that a walkout would begin at 10:30 A.M., and that management had not been informed of this action. Union leaders hoped that the shock of a sudden walkout would jar Pullman and his officers into serious negotiations. Now union loyalists wondered if the workforce would act together and walk off the job. A walkout that was not supported by a vast majority of workers would hurt the union's power at the bargaining table.

At exactly 10:30, union leaders put down their tools, turned off their machines, and stepped out of the factory doors. Dozens of other workers quietly did the same. The strikers gathered along Florence Boulevard and stood facing the factories to see how many other workers would join their movement. Hundreds poured out of the buildings with smiles of triumph on their faces. After a winter of unbearable suffering, they were now striking a blow by saying, "No more!" to the bosses. Onlookers on Florence Boulevard cheered as more and more employees walked out the doors. The

Despite the walkout and the strike, classes continued at the Pullman School.

loudest cheers came when the women of the Embroidery Department marched out as if they were on parade.

In all, some three thousand of Pullman's thirty-three hundred employees participated in the walkout on May 11, 1894. Company officials closed down the plants. That evening, a sign went up over the gates: "THE WORKS ARE CLOSED UNTIL FURTHER NOTICE."[4] The first act of the Pullman drama had begun.

Friends of the Strikers

Peace reigned in the weeks following the walkout as the strikers conducted themselves in a disciplined manner.

Pullman factory workers are seen here filing out of the main gate after the long work day.

Union leaders assigned men to act as guards and patrol the outsides of the factory complex. The guards discouraged angry employees from throwing bricks through windows or tearing down fences. Factory officials complained that these guards also intimidated any worker who wished to give up on the strike and return to his or her job.

As long as calm prevailed at Pullman, Illinois, the national mood seemed to favor the strikers. All dramas have villains. In the public eye, George Pullman was the rogue. It was true that many Americans feared that labor unions were getting too demanding and too violent. Yet they saw the Pullman strike as a David versus Goliath battle, and sided with the underdog.

Mayor John Hopkins of Chicago helped various charities raise fifteen thousand dollars to aid the strikers. Twenty-five hundred pounds of meat were donated to the union to help feed hungry workers. Doctors volunteered to treat sick Pullman employees without charge. Around Chicago men and women wore white ribbons on their wrists to display unity with the strikers.

Powerful and famous individuals also rallied behind the cause of the Pullman workers. Several of these men and women dominated the stage of this drama as if they were starring actors. One such star was John Peter Altgeld (1847–1902). Altgeld was born in Germany and came to the United States with his family when he was a child. He grew up in poverty and worked his way through school as a farm laborer. He then became a schoolteacher and later a lawyer and a politician. In 1892, Altgeld was elected governor of Illinois. One of his first acts as governor was to free the three men still held in prison for the 1886 Haymarket Massacre. Many believed the three were dangerous anarchists, and their release made Altgeld one of the most hated politicians in the country. But Altgeld reviewed the Haymarket trial and determined it was a farce. As long as he was governor no one would be held in prison if he or she had not had a fair trial.

Governor Altgeld visited the town of Pullman in the winter of 1893 and then wrote an angry letter to George Pullman:

I examined the conditions in Pullman yesterday, visited even the kitchens and bedrooms of many of the people. . . . The men are hungry and the women and children are actually suffering. . . . Men who had worked for your company for more than ten years had to apply to the relief society [for food and clothing]. . . . Something must be done and at once.[5]

George Pullman was unmoved by the governor's letter. Altgeld remained a friend of the Pullman workers during the trying times of the strike.

Another prominent character in the Pullman drama was Jane Addams. Addams was born to a prosperous family in the town of Cedarville, Illinois, in 1860. She was saddened when she saw poor children, barefoot and dressed in rags, wandering about her neighborhood. At an early age she dedicated her life to helping the poor. Addams moved to Chicago and established a settlement house, called Hull House, in the heart of an immigrant district. Hull House was a neighborhood center where classes were conducted, hungry people were fed, and children went for games and fun. Working mainly with immigrant women and children, Addams provided food and clothing and taught people job skills.

In Chicago society, Jane Addams served as a vital bridge between rich and poor communities. The rich admired her gentle manners, her education, and her intelligence. Poor people respected her devotion to their cause. Addams tried to make peace between Pullman and his workers but was frustrated in her efforts. She wrote, "I had known Mr. Pullman and had

Jane Addams was a famous social worker and a friend of the Pullman strikers.

seen his genuine pride and pleasure in the model town he had built with so much care."[6] Addams later compared Pullman to King Lear, the character in a famous Shakespeare play who allowed his own pride to destroy all he loved.

The most dynamic friend of the Pullman workers and one of the leading characters in the strike story was Eugene Debs. Normally a gentle man, he could display a fiery temper. Debs was furious when he went to Pullman during the walkout and saw hungry children. Debs was reluctant to lead his young union into battle

SOURCE DOCUMENT

THE FORCES OF LABOR MUST UNITE. THE DIVIDING LINES MUST GROW DIMMER DAY BY DAY UNTIL THEY BECOME IMPERCEPTIBLE, AND THEN LABOR'S HOSTS, MARSHALLED UNDER ONE CONQUERING BANNER, SHALL MARCH TOGETHER, VOTE TOGETHER AND FIGHT TOGETHER, UNTIL WORKINGMEN SHALL RECEIVE AND ENJOY ALL THE FRUITS OF THEIR TOIL. . . . SUCH AN ARMY WOULD BE IMPREGNABLE. NO CORPORATION WOULD ASSAIL IT. THE REIGN OF JUSTICE WOULD BE INAUGURATED. . . . AN ERA OF GOOD WILL AND PEACE WOULD DAWN.[7]

Eugene Debs harbored an ultimate dream to unite all workers—industrial and farm, men and women, black and white—into one nationwide organization. He was never able to achieve this dream, but he constantly pleaded for unity among working-class people. Standing six feet tall, lean and hard-muscled, he was a convincing speaker. Debs made this speech just weeks before the Pullman strike.

against George Pullman and his powerful friends in the railroad industry. Still, he could not contain his anger. At one meeting of Pullman workers, Debs said, "It is a fact that after working for George Pullman for years you appear . . . ragged and hungry [and this] only emphasizes the charge [that] Pullman stands before you a self-confessed robber."[8]

Unless you take decided action at once the riot and rebellion will be entirely beyond your control and much property and blood will have to be sacrificed and I fear we will never return to the peaceful years of the past. . . . No half hearted measures will satisfy any one. If an officer of the army with a regiment of soldiers are placed in charge [in Chicago] he should clear [every] striker and rioter or leave his men dead on the field as martyrs to liberty.

THE PULLMAN TRAGEDY

—From a letter written by a prominent Chicago businessman to Grover Cleveland, president of the United States, on July 6, 1894.[1]

Tensions Continue

The summer of 1894 broke over a nation seething with anger. Because of the stubborn depression, some 20 percent of the American workforce was jobless. Factory cities such as Chicago and Detroit faced unemployment figures as high as 50 percent. In those cities women and children were seen rummaging through garbage cans, looking for food. Many poor Americans blamed the railroads, the arteries of the Industrial Revolution, for the country's plight. In this atmosphere of tension the American Railway Union (ARU) met in Chicago for its first convention.

The Debs-led ARU embraced railroad workers in the Midwest region, and the union was naturally interested in the Pullman situation. Some delegates to the convention argued that they should refuse to work on trains that included Pullman cars. Such a boycott would leave Pullman passengers stranded on the tracks and would hopefully force the company into serious negotiations. Other delegates argued that the infant ARU was not strong enough to succeed in such a daring action.

On June 12, 1894, a Pullman seamstress named Jennie Curtis spoke to the convention. She was a thin, tired-looking woman who worked in Pullman's Embroidery Department. Her tear-choked words set the audience trembling with rage. Curtis's father had worked for the Pullman Company for thirteen years. He died, owing the company sixty dollars for rent on a tiny cottage. The Pullman Company deducted the back rent, bit by bit, from the five-dollar-a-week paycheck Jennie Curtis earned sewing fancy lace for Pullman dining cars. At the conclusion of Curtis's speech, the mostly male audience exploded into a chorus of curses. What a terrible injustice to this woman! How devilish of the Pullman Company to charge even the dead!

The convention sent the following message to the Pullman Company headquarters: "Unless the Pullman Palace Car Company does adjust the [workers'] grievances before June 26, 1894, the members of the American Railway Union shall refuse to handle

Pullman cars and equipment."[2] Pullman officials said there was nothing to negotiate. The Boycott, Act Two of the Pullman Drama, began.

The Boycott

On June 27, some five thousand railroad workers walked off their jobs to show sympathy with the Pullman employees. The next day, that number swelled to 125,000, and the day after that to 150,000. Such a vast industry-wide strike had never occurred before. The strikers represented ARU members of every craft—switchmen, firemen, brakemen, engineers, and laborers. Others who did not walk off their jobs announced that they would not work on any train that included a Pullman car. Twenty railroad lines over several midwestern states were tied up by the boycott. Overnight the busy freight yards in the Chicago area fell silent. The Chicago *Times* printed the headline, "Not a Wheel Turns in the West."[3]

Eugene Debs looked with pride at the number of railroad workers who participated in the work action. But he worried that he could not control the masses of angry men and women engaged in the strike. So far the public had been more or less on the side of the Pullman workers. However, the national mood grew edgy as train service was disrupted. Fear of an all-out war between rich and poor gripped the nation. Debs knew that fighting between railroad guards and strikers, or any sort of disorder, was likely to swing public opinion against the workers. He sent a strong message to all his followers: "Use no Violence."[4]

Debs's warnings were ignored. On June 30, crowds in Chicago placed huge steel beams on tracks and stopped an Illinois Central train. The crowd forced the Illinois Central crew to unhook two Pullman cars. Fistfights between union and nonunion men broke out in railroad yards in Indiana and Missouri. Mobs damaged railroad company property at Cairo, Illinois. It was unclear if the trouble was caused by the hands of ARU members or was simply the work of unemployed hooligans who hung around railroad yards. Violence— Eugene Debs's greatest fear—was beginning to emerge in the Pullman strike.

In those days, before radio and television, people relied on the newspapers to tell them of events taking place throughout the country. With growing interest Americans read accounts of the trouble brewing in Chicago. Newspapers soon became players in the Pullman story.

In ancient Greece, the audience at a theater heard a chorus that told them of subtle events and thoughts taking place beyond the words of the actors. The Pullman strike also had such a chorus in the press. Most newspapers were owned by wealthy families and relied on powerful companies for advertising. With few exceptions, newspapers—the Greek chorus of the Pullman drama—denounced the strikers. The *Chicago Tribune* wrote stories condemning "dictator Debs [and his] drunken followers."[5] Fear sells papers, and the press often exaggerated minor incidents and presented them as a violent insurrection. On June 30, 1894, a headline in the *Chicago Tribune* screamed, "THE MOB IS IN CONTROL."[6] This headline came despite the fact that Mayor John Hopkins and the city's chief of police insisted there was no widespread disorder anywhere in Chicago at that date.

If violence were to come, Chicago was a tinderbox that could set the entire Midwest aflame. The city was home to settled working people as well as to thousands of drifters who had come to claim temporary jobs at the World's Fair. In the summer of 1894, small armies

SOURCE DOCUMENT

THE ATTITUDE OF THE CHICAGO PRESS HAS BEEN SUCH AS TO COMPLETELY BEWILDER THE THOUGHTFUL AND INTELLIGENT CITIZEN WHO DESIRES TO KNOW THE TRUTH. . . . I PRESUME THAT IF I LIVED IN CHICAGO . . . AND KNEW NOTHING ABOUT THE PULLMAN STRIKE EXCEPT WHAT I READ IN THE THREE LEADING CHICAGO NEWSPAPERS, I WOULD HAVE RAISED MY HAND IN HOLY HORROR AGAINST THESE WICKED PULLMAN STRIKERS AND ALL BELONGING TO THEIR SIDE, AND WOULD HAVE SUSTAINED MR. PULLMAN AND HIS COMPANY. . . . BUT, LIVING AS I DO IN PULLMAN . . . I KNOW ENOUGH TO ENABLE ME TO READ BETWEEN THE LINES [OF THE NEWSPAPER STORIES] AND NOTE THE FALLACIES OF THEIR POSITION.[7]

The Reverend William Carwardine was a minister who preached in and around the town of Pullman. He saw the events of the strike unfold day by day and was dismayed by newspaper coverage that he believed was slanted against the workers. Writing after the strike, Carwardine made this statement.

of those temporary workers remained in the city, bored, broke, and looking for excitement.

The Battlelines Are Drawn

Debs and the ARU did not contend with the Pullman Palace Car Company alone. George Pullman was a member of a group of powerful railroad owners called the General Managers Association (GMA). The GMA represented twenty-four railroad companies centered in Chicago. All told, the GMA controlled 41,000 miles of track, had 220,000 employees, and owned property and machinery valued at more than $800 million. This mighty railroad organization actually looked forward to a fight with Debs and the ARU. The managers feared an industrywide union would gain too much strength. They hoped to defeat the union while it was still young and comparatively weak. The battle now pitted the ARU against GMA—workers against money.

Eugene Debs lamented the fact that his union was now set against the might of the railroad industry. Debs said,

> The struggle with the Pullman Company has developed into a contest between the producing classes and the money power of the country. . . . The fight was between the American Railway Union and the Pullman Company. . . . Then the railway corporations, through the General Managers Association came to the rescue and declared to the world that they would go into partnership with Pullman, so to speak, and stand by him in his devilish work of starving his employees to death.[8]

Making matters more difficult for the workers, the GMA would soon enlist another powerful ally: the United States government.

In the 1890s, almost all mail was carried overland by trains. Delivering the United States mail was a function of the federal government. Therefore, it could be concluded, the disruption of train service halted mail delivery and was an act that defied national authority. Eugene Debs and other ARU leaders were aware that interfering with the mail could lead to serious charges against the union. Debs instructed striking workers to leave mail cars alone. But the GMA, hoping to draw the federal government into the dispute, made sure that there was at least one mail car attached to every Pullman train going in and out of Chicago. When those trains were stopped by strikers, the federal government became a force in the Pullman Strike.

Enter an additional character in the drama shaking the nation. Richard Olney (1835–1917) was born in Oxford, Massachusetts, and graduated from Harvard Law School. As a young lawyer, he lost cases because his cold and coarse mannerisms alienated juries. So he worked behind the scenes as a corporate lawyer. Most of his clients were powerful railroad companies. Always interested in politics, Olney was a ranking member of the Democratic party. In 1893, President Grover Cleveland appointed Olney as the United States attorney general, the chief law enforcement officer of the federal government.

To Olney, the strikers in Chicago were interfering with the mail, and consequently, breaking the law. He would hear no counterarguments. Lawyers working for Olney went to court and secured an injunction (a court order) to protect mail delivery. The injunction said that any worker who refused to service a train carrying a mail car was violating the law. Under the best of circumstances a striking railroad union would have difficulty obeying this injunction, especially given the GMA policy of attaching mail cars to most Pullman trains. With rage increasing among workers, compliance with the court order proved impossible. The injunction was ignored by the ARU. Workers refused to handle Pullman trains whether or not they included mail cars.

Attorney General Olney sprang into action. He made public statements claiming he must safeguard the mails and that he intended to punish all those who violated the court order. Olney persuaded President Grover Cleveland to send United States Army troops to Chicago. The bulk of the troops came from nearby Fort Sheridan. Some six thousand strong, the soldiers pitched tents at Grant Park on the city's lakefront. Chicagoans watched in shock as teams of horses pulled cannons down the middle of Michigan Avenue. The sudden appearance of the army unsettled the nation. Chicago was an American city, not some European village where the king's guards were regularly called in to terrorize the people.

Illinois Governor John Peter Altgeld was furious. He had not asked for soldiers to come to his state. Normally, federal troops were sent to states only to quell a riot. Even then, the soldiers had to be requested by the governor. Altgeld had made no such request. He insisted that the state militia and the Chicago police force had the situation well in hand. Altgeld sent a telegram to President Cleveland condemning the intervention of federal troops as an action that was "unnecessary [and] unjustifiable."[9] Still, the troops stayed.

Not content with having the army camped in Chicago, the GMA hired private security guards of its own. The guards, many of whom were drifters who had come to the city for the World's Fair, were given guns and badges. They were taken to freight yards where they were ordered to protect railroad property. They were paid $2.50 a day, considerably more than the railroads paid laborers. The federal government also deputized temporary marshals who were to serve as peacekeepers. The railroads paid the marshals and provided them with guns. In all, five thousand men were sworn in as guards or as marshals. Looking over the ranks of these new law enforcement officers, a reporter from the Chicago *Herald* observed, "They were a very low, contemptible set of men."[10]

In the first days of July 1894, Chicago had the look of a city at war. Fourteen thousand armed men had taken positions in various parts of the town. These included five thousand guards and marshals, six thousand troops, and three thousand policemen. Unemployed and hungry workers looked upon the armed men as an occupying army designed to suppress the lower classes. Eugene Debs walked the streets of Chicago, and told a reporter,

> The first shots fired by the regular soldiers at mobs here will be the signal for a civil war. I believe this as firmly as I believe in the ultimate success of our course. Bloodshed will follow and ninety per cent of the people of the United States will be arrayed [ready to fight] against the other ten per cent. And I would not care to be arrayed against the laboring people in this contest.[11]

RECEIVING AND QUESTIONING APPLICANTS FOR APPOINTMENTS AS DEPUTIES AT THE MARSHAL'S OFFICE, CHICAGO.

CHICAGO AND NORTHWESTERN RAILROAD ROUND-HOUSE, JULY 3, 1894—NOT AN ENGINE MOVING.

DEPUTIES TRYING TO MOVE AN ENGINE AND CAR ON THE CHICAGO, ROCK ISLAND, AND PACIFIC RAILROAD AT BLUE ISLAND, JULY 2, 1894.

THE GREAT RAILWAY STRIKES—SCENES IN AND ABOUT CHICAGO.—FROM SKETCHES BY G. A. COFFIN.—[SEE PAGE 655.]

These three drawings appeared in magazines during the Pullman strike, describing the impact the strike had, even beyond Chicago.

The Fourth of July would normally be a day of patriotic parades and picnics. Instead, the Fourth dawned on a city alive with tension. Trouble broke out that night at the Union Stock Yards, long a hotbed of labor unrest. Gangs of young ruffians who seemed to be itching for a fight broke down stockyard fences and set fire to the hay that was meant for cattle feed. Rioting spread throughout the South Side. Several abandoned buildings on the old World's Fair grounds were torched. They went up in a spectacular blaze that turned night into day. An observer named Ray Baker reported, "All southern Chicago seemed afire. I saw long freight trains burning on side tracks. I saw attacks by strikers on nonunion men, and fierce conflicts between strikers and the police and deputies."[12]

During the riotous night, guards shot at mobs, and at least two people were killed. The heart of the trouble sprang up miles from the village of Pullman, and no Pullman workers had been injured. Yet shots were fired and the first blood had been spilled in the Pullman strike.

Riot!

"Panic Reigns In Chicago," read one New York City headline on July 5.[13] The *New York Herald* wrote about "Mobs thirsty for blood . . ."[14] In an editorial, the *Chicago Tribune* warned strikers that with the army in town, they "will be fired upon, they will be bayoneted, they will be trampled under foot by cavalry, and mowed down by artillery."[15]

Governor John Altgeld dismissed the sensational newspaper accounts, but he could not deny that the Pullman strike was taking an ugly turn. Altgeld called the Illinois state militia to Chicago, and the federal government sent even more troops. In Washington, President Grover Cleveland repeated the government's vow to protect the mail. Cleveland said, "If it takes every dollar in the Treasury and every soldier in the United States Army to deliver a postal card in Chicago, the postal card will be delivered."[16]

Act Three of the Pullman drama—the July Riot—had begun.

Guards armed with pistols rode on the sides of train engines and sat on the cowcatchers that protruded from the front. As the trains passed through working-class neighborhoods, the guards were pelted with stones. During the confrontations, the guards and the workers passed whiskey bottles among themselves and took deep drinks to bolster their courage. Newspaper stories claimed that the mobs of workers were crazy drunk, but one reporter from the Chicago *Record* declared, "I must say that I saw more deputy sheriffs and deputy marshals drunk than I saw strikers drunk."[17]

In two separate incidents on July 7, 1894, state militia troops fired into crowds who were cursing them and hurling stones. Four people were killed and more than forty wounded. None of the killed or injured rioters were ARU members. Debs had remarkable control over his men. He told unionists to stay home and stay clear of the rioting. The vast majority of

In this artist's depiction, troops protect trains at the Chicago stockyards during the rioting.

them obeyed their leader. After the shooting incidents on July 7, Debs said in a speech, "We have repeatedly declared that we will respect law and order. . . . A man who commits violence in any form, whether a member of our order or not, should be promptly arrested and punished."[18]

Still, violence exploded in the city. On the South Side, soldiers dismounted from a train engine and launched a bayonet charge against rioters. Shots rang out in many neighborhoods. Scattered fires broke out. Innocent people as well as rioters were killed and wounded. In nearby Hammond, Indiana, a father went to look for his young son who had wandered out of the yard. The father found himself near the railroad tracks in the midst of a mob of people who shouted and shook their fists at guards. Shots were fired. The father lay bleeding to death near the tracks.

The worst rioting took place over July 6 and 7, when it seemed that all the hungry and desperate masses of Chicago descended on railroad yards in various parts of the city. Cars carrying food were hit first. Rioters broke open the doors of freightcars. They carried off huge cuts of meat and sacks of potatoes. Where guards were present, fights broke out. Shots rang in the air and people scattered, screaming. When guards retreated the mobs returned. Pushing together, scores of men overturned boxcars. More than seven hundred cars were destroyed in the city. Everywhere fires were set. It appeared to some observers that a second Chicago fire would level the city.

Soldiers guard the streets of Pullman during the strike.

Finally, from sheer exhaustion, the rioters quieted down. As calm was restored, Eugene Debs and several other union leaders were arrested for violating a court order and for interfering with the mail. Working people were outraged by the arrests. Some labor leaders called for a general strike, for every worker in Chicago to walk off the job and stay off until Debs and the others were freed. But the spirit of the workers was broken after the days and nights of rioting. The general strike lasted a day or so. Then people went to work as usual. Most workers were depressed. They believed the Pullman strike was a tragic defeat for the American labor movement.

The public should not permit the real question which has been before it to be obscured. That question was the creation of a dictatorship which could make all the industries of the United States . . . hostages for the granting of the fantastic whim of the dictator. Any submission to him [Debs] would have been a long step in that direction.

THE AFTERMATH

—A statement issued by George Pullman shortly after the strike.[1]

The Trial

A headline in the *Chicago Tribune* said it all: "DEBS' STRIKE IS DEAD."[2] The smoke cleared, tempers cooled, and the army left Chicago. Once more trains moved freely. Surprisingly, there was very little damage in the town of Pullman. The Pullman workers, who had been largely forgotten in the violence and rioting, now quietly went back to work for the same wages and under the old rent conditions. The most vocal Pullman unionists were fired. Others had to sign a pledge that they would not join union activities in the future.

Though the Pullman strike was centered in Chicago, it had upset the entire nation. With amazing swiftness the strike spread to the western states. Union men as far away as Sacramento, California, and Butte, Montana, refused to handle trains that carried Pullman cars. In an alarming form of sabotage, union sympathizers blew up railroad bridges in what was then the Oklahoma Territory. Comfortable Americans were terrified by the strike's violent turn. Many blamed Eugene Debs for the disorder that was often called "Debs Rebellion."[3] A teacher in New York City ordered her class to conduct a debate entitled, "Why Eugene Debs is the most dangerous man in America?"[4] In this atmosphere, the trial of Eugene Debs and the other union leaders began.

Enter Clarence Darrow, yet another actor on the Pullman strike stage. Clarence Darrow (1857–1938) was born in Ohio and attended the University of Michigan Law School. A Chicago resident, he worked as a lawyer for the Chicago and Northwestern Railroad. Outraged by the way the railroads treated workers during the Pullman strike, he resigned his position and defended Eugene Debs in court. This proved to be a difficult task. Debs was charged by the federal government with violating a court order and interfering with the mail, both serious offenses. He was held in the darkest basement of Cook County Jail with the city's most dangerous murderers and thieves. Debs claimed that sewer rats the size of cats regularly scurried across the floor of his jail cell.

In court Darrow reviewed the union's conduct of the strike. He pointed out to the jury that the ARU had no intention of disrupting the mails because union

Clarence Darrow served as Eugene Debs's lawyer in the controversial case after the Pullman strike.

members did not refuse to handle all mail cars, only those that were attached to trains carrying Pullman vehicles. He also called witnesses who claimed that many violent street fights were started by the guards and special deputies hired by the railroads.

Despite Darrow's eloquence, he lost his battle. A federal judge sentenced Eugene Debs to six months in jail. Debs was transferred to a prison in Woodstock, Illinois, some fifty miles outside of Chicago. Often during his prison term, Debs's Chicago supporters journeyed to Woodstock and sang songs under his cell window. Debs was released from jail on November 22, 1895, a bitter cold day when snow covered the streets. Despite the nasty weather, Debs was welcomed at the train station by one hundred thousand cheering Chicagoans.

The Characters

The trial of Eugene Debs and other union leaders was the fourth and final act of the Pullman strike drama. However, its characters continued to make their marks in American history.

Eugene Debs emerged from the strike a changed man. During his six months in prison, Debs busied himself reading. He pored over the works of American social reformers such as Henry George and Edward Bellamy. Those writers dreamed of building a new and glorious society based on common ownership of important industries such as railroads, steel, and large farms. Debs entered jail a labor leader and came out a Socialist.

His newfound love for socialism and humanism (concern for people's rights) can be seen in the lines of this poem he penned while behind bars:

> *While there is a lower class I am in it;*
> *While there is a criminal element I am of it;*
> *While there is a soul in prison I am not free.*[5]

During the long prison nights, Debs determined that the government would always side with business in labor disputes. Therefore, if workers were to make gains they must change the government. Socialism, he believed, was the answer. Debs was one of the founders of the American Socialist party. He ran for president under that party's banner five times. In 1920, he received almost a million votes for president, even though at the time he was confined to jail for protesting American involvement in World War I. Debs today is hailed as one of the most courageous radical leaders in American history.

Debs's lawyer, Clarence Darrow, went on to defend many unpopular causes. He became a champion of the underdog. He believed that everyone deserved a decent lawyer, no matter what terrible crime he or she was accused of committing. He defended political rebels and African Americans charged with crimes against whites. He was a staunch opponent of the death penalty. One of Darrow's most famous cases came in 1925 when he was the lawyer for two wealthy young men, Richard Loeb and Nathan Leopold. The two had brutally murdered a fourteen-year-old boy simply for the thrill of the crime. Darrow made an impassioned plea to save the lives of the murderers and succeeded in getting them a life sentence. Also in 1925, Darrow participated in the famous "Scopes Monkey Trial," where he defended Tennessee high school teacher John Scopes, who had been accused of breaking a state law by lecturing on evolution. Today, Darrow is praised as a lawyer-hero who devoted his life to what were seemingly lost causes.

Throughout the Pullman strike, Jane Addams worked tirelessly to restore peace between George Pullman, whom she knew and liked, and his workers. She failed to achieve an accord, but the Pullman strike established Addams as one of the great movers for change during the Gilded Age. For the rest of her life she led community groups that demanded cleaner streets in the cities and safer working conditions in the factories. She was a major voice in the drive to secure voting rights for women, and she was a determined foe of war. In 1931, she won the Nobel Peace Prize, the first woman to achieve that award. When she died in 1935, Addams was one of the most celebrated women in the United States.

Illinois Governor John Peter Altgeld was also a friend to the workers, and he paid a price for his loyalty. From the beginning, Altgeld insisted that there was no need to send federal troops to Chicago during the Pullman strike. He further claimed that the presence of the soldiers fanned the flames of violence on city streets. During the strike, newspapers blasted Altgeld for his stand. A magazine called *The Nation* said

Altgeld was the "friend and champion of disorder."[6] In an editorial on July 7, 1894, the *Chicago Tribune* claimed, "This lying, hypocritical, demagogical [given to fiery speeches], sniveling governor of Illinois does not want the law enforced."[7] Altgeld was defeated when he ran for re-election in 1896. He died six years later, still a figure of scorn in most of the country. Today, however, many historians hail Altgeld as one of the most courageous politicians of his time.

Historians have less kind things to say about Richard Olney, the attorney general of the United States. Olney harbored a personal hatred for Eugene Debs. He successfully argued against Debs when Debs appealed his Pullman strike conviction to the United States Supreme Court. In 1895, President Grover Cleveland appointed Olney as secretary of state. In that capacity, Olney helped resolve the Venezuela Boundary Dispute, a bitter argument between Venezuela and Great Britain. Olney left public office for good in 1897, but he remained an active voice in the Democratic party. Many historians believe the Pullman strike hurt Olney, President Cleveland, and the Democratic party. In the election of 1896, the Republicans regained the presidency and won a majority of seats in Congress.

Finally, there is George Pullman, the truly tragic figure of the Pullman strike story. During the strike, Pullman was strangely silent. He spent most of the violent days of July at his summer home on the seashore in Elberon, New Jersey. But clearly the strike upset him. He lost weight. Friends said he was oddly ill-tempered and looked as if he were having problems sleeping. George Pullman died of a heart attack on October 19, 1897, just three years after the great strike. He was sixty-six years old. Eugene Debs commented, "Peace be to his ashes. . . . He [Pullman] is on an equality with his toilers now."[8]

George Pullman's ideas made long-distance train travel comfortable for millions of passengers. Starting from nothing, he built one of the most powerful companies in the world. His greatest pride was the supposedly ideal town he constructed for his workers. It is true that he created the town on the theory that a happy worker is a good worker, and proper employee housing

George Pullman was buried in the Pullman family gravesite at Graceland Cemetery in Chicago.

would pay off in greater productivity. Aside from the profit motive, however, George Pullman built houses that were among the best in the world, judged by the standards of working-class dwellings of the 1880s. The workers' revolt was, to Pullman, the ultimate act of ingratitude, a terrible slap in the face to a man who believed he had given his employees so much.

George M. Pullman is often portrayed as the demon in the strike story. It is easy to characterize him in such a manner. He was not a genial or a particularly friendly man. Making money seemed to be his chief pleasure. Yet he often said—and he probably believed—that he wanted only the best for his workers. His problem was stubbornness. The depression of 1893 was a blow to all working people. Pullman, as the owner of both the factory and the town, could have softened the blow for his own employees. Instead, he adamantly refused to adjust workers' rents in the wake of falling wages. He did this despite the fact the Pullman Palace Car Company made money during the depression.

When Pullman died, his family feared angry workers would dig up his coffin and desecrate the body. His funeral was held in private and at night. His body was taken secretly to Graceland Cemetery on Chicago's North Side. His was no ordinary grave. Cemetery workers dug a pit bigger than the average living room. After the coffin was deposited, it was covered with tons and tons of quick-drying concrete. It was announced that this extraordinary step was taken so that no anarchist would disturb Pullman's final resting place. But writer Ambrose Bierce had other ideas concerning the measure. "It is clear," said Bierce, "the family in its bereavement was making sure [he] wasn't going to get up and come back."[9]

The Legacy

The violence of the Pullman strike shocked the American people, especially because it came at a time when labor unrest was sweeping the country. In the late 1800s, the public saw the bloody railroad strike in West Virginia, the Haymarket Riot, the steel strike in Homestead, Pennsylvania, the march of Coxey's Army, and dozens of other clashes between rich and poor. Many Americans feared the Pullman strike would be the terrible trigger to ignite civil war in the land.

In many respects, the Pullman strike was the most important labor dispute in United States history. It set the tone for the twentieth-century labor movement. On the surface, the strike was a crushing blow for unions. The Pullman workers went back to their jobs having gained nothing. The American Railway Union (ARU), Debs's dream of an industrywide organization, broke up soon after the strike. It was feared that organized labor would never survive the Pullman defeat.

In fact, the Pullman strike only caused the goals of labor to change direction. Gone were the dreams of Debs and others to form one giant organization of workers. Instead the labor movement reverted back to trade groups. Unions in general now worked for limited goals and specific changes. Samuel Gompers's American Federation of Labor (AFL) concentrated on wages and working conditions. The AFL became the most successful labor union in the twentieth century.

Why this change? Why did the Pullman strike dash the hopes of those who believed that working people could unite in one vast union and give the lower classes power over the rich? Most historians believe the action of the government in the Pullman strike caused the shift in direction for the labor movement. All too willingly, the government joined forces with Pullman and the railroad managers. The government's weapon was the court injunction. In the Pullman strike, the injunction told workers that failing to handle trains with mail cars attached was a violation of the law. Ironically, this injunction was based on the Sherman Anti-Trust Act, a law that was designed to break up large corporations. Labor leaders now feared that the government could use broad court injunctions to put down any strike. For this reason, unions sought more limited goals.

After George Pullman died, his trusted attorney Robert Todd Lincoln took over the company. A competent businessman, Robert Todd was President Abraham Lincoln's only surviving son. The firm thrived under his leadership. For years to come, the Pullman Company built outstanding passenger cars for railroads around the world.

Lincoln continued the company policy of using African Americans as porters on Pullman trains. This practice produced an interesting aside in American history. In the 1890s, the vast majority of African Americans lived in the Southern states. Chicago, for example, was less than one percent black, according to the 1890 census. Then African-American Pullman porters began spreading the word that Southern African Americans could gain new opportunities and greater freedoms in the North. Some porters distributed African-American-owned newspapers such as the Chicago *Defender*, which urged African Americans to move to the Northern states. In this small way, Pullman Company porters helped start the great migration of African Americans to the North that took place early in the twentieth century.

The town of Pullman remained as a testament to the vision of its founder. In 1907, a court acted to reduce the power the company had over its employees, and ordered the company to sell its houses to individual owners. Pullman is now a Chicago South Side neighborhood spreading over thirty-five blocks and holding some four thousand residents. A devastating fire in 1998 leveled much of the old factory complex, but other monuments remain—the Greenstone Church, the Hotel Florence, and the rows of brick houses. It is generally a happy neighborhood where residents are proud of their community and its history. Preservationists strive to keep the unique architecture of the community intact.

On almost any day visitors walk the streets of Pullman. Many are history buffs. Some come from

This photo of the Hotel Florence, the showcase building in Pullman, Illinois, was taken in the 1890s. It remains a centerpiece of the former town, now a tourist attraction.

Today, visitors can still see the town of Pullman, and learn about the history of its failure to become a perfect community of happy workers.

overseas just to see this planned village, now more than one hundred years old. While strolling about the streets, they try to imagine the excitement, the passion, and the fear generated by the great strike. The 1894 upheaval was a tragedy in which dreams were shattered and lives lost. But it was also a drama filled with larger-than-life characters, a drama that made an impact on the nation for generations to come.

★ TIMELINE ★

Early 1800s—The Industrial Revolution begins in the United States.

1831—George Pullman is born on March 3 in Brocton, New York.

1855—Eugene Debs is born on November 5 in Terre Haute, Indiana.

1858—Pullman buys two passenger cars and begins to convert them to sleeping cars.

1864—Pullman completes work on the Pioneer, a new sleeping car that allows passengers to ride in luxury.

1865—President Abraham Lincoln is assassinated; His body is taken from Chicago to Springfield, Illinois, aboard Pullman's Pioneer.

1867—Pullman organizes the Pullman Palace Car Company.

1869—The transcontinental railroad is completed, but it takes five to seven days to ride from New York to San Francisco aboard the fastest trains of the time; Such lengthy trips reinforce the need for comfortable passenger facilities.

1875—Eugene Debs joins the Brotherhood of Locomotive Firemen, his first labor union.

1879—Pullman purchases three thousand acres of land south of Chicago as a site for his model town.

1880—Work on the model town, called Pullman, Illinois, begins.

1885—Pullman, Illinois, is completed and holds a factory complex and almost nine thousand residents.

1886—A bomb thrown at police in Chicago's Haymarket Square kills ten people and rocks the nation.

1893—An economic depression strikes the country, throwing millions of people out of work.

June: Eugene Debs organizes the American Railway Union (ARU).

September: Because of the depression, George Pullman lowers the wages of his workers by 25 percent, but refuses to lower their rents.

1894—*January*: Many Pullman families face near starvation.

May 7: A committee of Pullman union members meets with management.

May 10: Three union leaders are fired without explanation.

May 11: Pullman workers go on strike.

June 26: The ARU announces that its members will not handle trains with Pullman cars attached to them.

June 30: Fights between railroad workers and guards break out in Blue Island and Cairo, Illinois.

July 2: Attorney General Richard Olney secures a court order that requires railroad workers to service trains carrying United States mail.

July 3: Federal troops arrive in Chicago over the objection of Governor John Altgeld.

July 4: Rioting breaks out in the Chicago stockyards; Most of the rioters are not railroad workers.

July 6–7: Fierce rioting jolts Chicago.

July 7: Eugene Debs and other union leaders are arrested for violating the court order secured by Richard Olney.

July 10: An uneasy peace prevails in Chicago.

August: The strike collapses, and most Pullman employees return to work under the same pay and rent conditions as before.

1895—*February*: Eugene Debs is sentenced to six months in jail.

1897—*October 19*: George Pullman dies at the age of sixty-six.

1907—A court orders the Pullman Company to sell its houses to private individuals.

1971—Pullman, now a Chicago neighborhood, is declared a National Historic Landmark.

1998—A fire destroys much of Pullman's old factory complex.

★ CHAPTER NOTES ★

Chapter 1. Setting the Stage

1. Almont Lindsey, *The Pullman Strike* (Chicago: The University of Chicago Press, 1964), p. 208.

Chapter 2. A Man and His Dream

1. Stanley Buder, *Pullman An Experiment in Industrial Order and Community Planning 1880–1930* (New York: Oxford University Press, 1967), p. 13.

2. Dee Brown, *Hear That Lonesome Whistle Blow* (New York: Holt, Rinehart, and Winston, 1977), p. 26.

3. Buder, p. 10.

4. Irving Stone, *Clarence Darrow for the Defense* (New York: Doubleday, 1941), p. 39.

5. Donald Miller, *City of the Century, The Epic of Chicago and the Making of America* (New York: Simon & Schuster, 1996), p. 234.

6. Almont Lindsey, *The Pullman Strike* (Chicago: The University of Chicago Press, 1964), p. 48.

7. Buder, p. 31.

8. Miller, p. 228.

Chapter 3. The Gilded Age

1. Carl Sandburg, *The American Songbag* (New York: Harcourt Brace, 1927), p. 195.

2. Stephen Longstreet, *Chicago 1860–1919* (New York: David McKay Company, Inc., 1973), p. 427.

3. Ray Ginger, *The Bending Cross, a Biography of Eugene Debs* (New Brunswick, N.J.: Rutgers University Press, 1949), p. 113.

4. Jane Addams, *Twenty Years at Hull-House* (Urbana, Ill.: University of Illinois Press, 1990), p. 103.

5. William Cahn, *A Pictorial History of American Labor* (New York: Crown Publishers, 1972), p. 143.

6. *The Annals of America* (Chicago: Encyclopaedia Britannica, Inc., 1976), vol. 11, p. 122.

7. Arthur M. Schlesinger, Jr., ed., *The Almanac of American History* (New York: Barnes & Noble Books, 1993), p. 361.

8. Donald Miller, *City of the Century, The Epic of Chicago and the Making of America* (New York: Simon & Schuster, 1996), p. 475.

9. Richard O. Boyer and Herbert M. Morais, *Labor's Untold Story* (New York: United Electrical Workers of America, 1955), p. 254.

Chapter 4. Solidarity Forever

1. *United Auto Workers Local 802*, n.d., <http://www.odyssey.subscribers/uaw/rel> (May 1999).

2. William Cahn, *A Pictorial History of American Labor* (New York: Crown Publishers, 1972), p. 117.

3. Ibid., p. 139.

4. *The Annals of America* (Chicago: Encyclopaedia Britannica, Inc., 1976), vol. 10, pp. 561–562.

5. Bernard A. Weisberger, *The Life History of the United States* (Alexandria, Va.: Time-Life Books, 1964), vol. 7, p. 86.

6. Ronald Radosh, ed., *Debs—Great Lives Observed* (Englewood Cliffs, N.J.: Prentice Hall, 1971), p. 97.

7. Ray Ginger, *The Bending Cross, a Biography of Eugene Debs* (New Brunswick, N.J.: Rutgers University Press, 1949), p. 19.

8. Ibid., p. 55.

Chapter 5. Trouble in Paradise

1. Richard O. Boyer and Herbert M. Morais, *Labor's Untold Story* (New York: United Electrical Workers of America, 1955), p. 124.

2. Almont Lindsey, *The Pullman Strike* (Chicago: The University of Chicago Press, 1964), p. 48.

3. William Cahn, *A Pictorial History of American Labor* (New York: Crown Publishers, 1972), p. 173.

4. Stephen Longstreet, *Chicago 1860–1919* (New York: David McKay Company, Inc., 1973), p. 428.

5. Lindsey, p. 91.

6. Donald Miller, *City of the Century, The Epic of Chicago and the Making of America* (New York: Simon & Schuster, 1996), p. 238.

7. Irving Stone, *Clarence Darrow for the Defense* (New York: Doubleday, 1941), p. 40.

8. Miller, p. 488.

9. Ibid., p. 534.

10. Lindsey, p. 94.

11. William Carwardine, *The Pullman Strike* (Chicago: Charles H. Kerr Publishing Company, 1994), p. 86.

12. Stanley Buder, *Pullman An Experiment in Industrial Order and Community Planning 1880–1930* (New York: Oxford University Press, 1967), p. 135.

13. Carl Smith, *Urban Disorder and the Shape of Belief* (Chicago: The University of Chicago Press, 1995), p. 235.

14. Richard Schneirov, Shelton Stormquist, and Nick Salvatore, eds., *The Pullman Strike and the Crises of the 1890s* (Urbana, Ill.: University of Illinois Press, 1999), p. 8.

Chapter 6. The Walkout

1. Almont Lindsey, *The Pullman Strike* (Chicago: The University of Chicago Press, 1964), p. 101.

2. Ibid., p. 102.

3. William Carwardine, *The Pullman Strike* (Chicago: Charles H. Kerr Publishing Company, 1994), p. 34.

4. Lindsey, p. 123.

5. William Cahn, *A Pictorial History of American Labor* (New York: Crown Publishers, 1972), p. 174.

6. Jane Addams, *Twenty Years At Hull-House* (Urbana, Ill.: University of Illinois Press, 1990), p. 126.

7. Ray Ginger, *The Bending Cross, a Biography of Eugene Debs* (New Brunswick, N.J.: Rutgers University Press, 1949), p. 115.

8. Ibid., p. 114.

Chapter 7. The Pullman Tragedy

1. Almont Lindsey, *The Pullman Strike* (Chicago: The University of Chicago Press, 1964), p. 211.

2. Stanley Buder, *Pullman An Experiment in Industrial Order and Community Planning 1880–1930* (New York: Oxford University Press, 1967), p. 179.

3. Carl Smith, *Urban Disorder and the Shape of Belief* (Chicago: The University of Chicago Press, 1995), p. 235.

4. Ray Ginger, *The Bending Cross, a Biography of Eugene Debs* (New Brunswick, N.J.: Rutgers University Press, 1949), p. 123.

5. Donald Miller, *City of the Century, The Epic of Chicago and the Making of America* (New York: Simon & Schuster, 1996), p. 545.

6. Ginger, p. 126.

7. William Carwardine, *The Pullman Strike* (Chicago: Charles H. Kerr Publishing Company, 1994), p. 48.

8. Ginger, p. 128.

9. Lindsey, p. 185.

10. Ibid., p. 167.

11. Ginger, p. 138.

12. Miller, p. 544.

13. Richard O. Boyer and Herbert M. Morais, *Labor's Untold Story* (New York: United Electrical Workers of America, 1955), p. 129.

14. Ibid.

15. Miller, p. 545.

16. Ginger, p. 137.

17. Lindsey, p. 167.

18. Ginger, p. 143.

Chapter 8. The Aftermath

1. Ray Ginger, *The Bending Cross, a Biography of Eugene Debs* (New Brunswick, N.J.: Rutgers University Press, 1949), p. 150.

2. Ibid.

3. Irving Stone, *Clarence Darrow for the Defense* (New York: Doubleday, 1941), p. 51.

4. Ibid., p. 52.

5. Page Smith, *The Rise of Industrial America* (New York: McGraw-Hill, 1984), vol. 6, p. 521.

6. Almont Lindsey, *The Pullman Strike* (Chicago: The University of Chicago Press, 1964), p. 192.

7. Ibid.

8. Ibid., p. 342.

9. Stephen Longstreet, *Chicago 1860–1919* (New York: David McKay Company, Inc., 1973), p. 432.

★ FURTHER READING ★

Books

Altman, Linda Jacobs. *The Pullman Strike of 1894: Turning Point for American Labor*. Brookfield, Conn.: Millbrook Press, 1994.

Carwardine, William. *The Pullman Strike*. Chicago: Charles H. Kerr Publishing Company, 1994.

Colman, Penny. *Strike! The Bitter Struggle of American Workers From Colonial Times to the Present*. Brookfield, Conn.: Millbrook Press, 1995.

Driemen, John E. *Clarence Darrow*. New York: Chelsea House Publishers, 1992.

Harvey, Bonnie Carman. *Jane Addams: Nobel Prize Winner and Founder of Hull House*. Berkeley Heights, N.J.: Enslow Publishers, Inc., 1999.

Kent, Deborah. *Jane Addams*. Danbury, Conn.: Children's Press, 1992.

McCormick, Anita Louise. *The Industrial Revolution in American History*. Springfield, N.J.: Enslow Publishers, Inc., 1998.

McPherson, Stephanie. *Peace and Bread: The Story of Jane Addams*. Minneapolis, Minn.: Carolrhoda Books, 1993.

Miller, Donald. *City of the Century, the Epic of Chicago and the Making of America*. New York: Simon & Schuster, 1996.

Schneirov, Richard; Stormquist, Shelton; and Nick Salvatore, eds. *The Pullman Strike and the Crises of the 1890s*. Urbana, Ill.: University of Illinois Press, Illinois, 1999.

Simonds, Patricia. *The Founding of the AFL and the Rise of Organized Labor*. Parsippany, N.J.: Silver Burdett, 1991.

Smith, Carl. *Urban Disorder and the Shape of Belief*. Chicago: The University of Chicago Press, 1995.

Stein, R. Conrad. *The Transcontinental Railroad in American History*. Springfield, N.J.: Enslow Publishers, Inc., 1997.

Internet Addresses

Chicago Public Library. "1894: The Pullman Strike." *Chicago Historical Information*. n.d. <http://cpl.lib.uic.edu/ 004chicago/disasters/pullman_strike.html> (June 14, 2000).

The Historic Pullman Foundation. *The Pullman Historic District*. n.d. <http://www.lincolnnet.net/users/lrhpf/ home.htm> (June 14, 2000).

Illinois State Museum. "United States Strike Commission: The Pullman Strike: Its Causes and Events." *At Home in a House Divided: 1850–1890*. December 31, 1996. <http:// www.museum.state.il.us/exhibits/athome/1850/voices/ curtis/strike.htm> (June 14, 2000).

PBS Online. "Carnivals of Revenge." *The American Experience*. 1999. <http://www.pbs.org/wgbh/amex/ carnegie/revenge.html> (June 14, 2000).

★ INDEX ★